WHERE YOU FROM?

TALES OF SANDTOWN

ALBERT PHILLIPS JR.

2025

Copyright © 2025 by Albert Phillips Jr.

All rights reserved. No part of this book may be reproduced, distributed, or transmitted in any form or by any means, including photocopying, recording, or other electronic or mechanical methods, without the prior written permission of the publisher, except in the case of brief quotations embodied in reviews, critical articles, or certain other noncommercial uses permitted by copyright law. For permission requests, contact the publisher at the address below.

Free Black Mind Educational Group LLC
P.O. Box 6250 Baltimore, Maryland 21206

www.AlbertPhillipsJr.com

For bulk copies and book-related events, please email hello@albertphillipsjr.com.

ISBNs:
Print: 978-1-7353247-4-6
eBook: 978-1-7353247-5-3
Library of Congress Catalog Card # 2025921721

Edited by Laurie Willis Davis www.laurieswritetouch.com
Cover design and chapter title images by Morgan Elliott
Interior design by Nikiea Redmond, Publish Your Way

Printed in the United States of America

Note: Some names and identifying details have been changed to protect the privacy of individuals.

A version of the essay "We Fit the Description" was previously published in Towson University's Grub Street, Volume 74.

The poem "Concrete Rapunzel" by Denim Fisher is included in this collection with permission.

First Edition

As Benny the Butcher once rapped, my gift for turning words into imagery is what will make people remember me. (paraphrased)

To my sweet grandmother, Delores Noble
I miss you and love you so much, and I am forever thankful to know that you were proud of me when you took your last breath.

PREFACE

In Baltimore, there's one question no native can avoid: Where you from?

It's more than small talk. It's a check. A subtle scan of your foundation. If you say you're homegrown, people want to know where your roots are buried. They want to know who raised you, what corners taught you and what high school molded you. It's a conversation I've never been fully comfortable with because my roots are spread throughout the city. Still, nobody lets you skip it. Sooner or later, you've got to stand on something.

Sometimes, I say I'm from Sandtown-Winchester. Not because I was born there or because my name rings bells in that part of town, but because it's the place that raised questions in me about my identity, voice and worthiness. Sandtown-Winchester is the place that held me when I didn't even know I needed to be held. My father was still learning how to be a dad, reshaping himself after gaining custody of me. And I was a newly motherless boy, still trying to find my balance as a young Black kid in a world that rarely showed empathy for Black fathers and their sons.

I lived there for only four years. But in those years, I learned more about the world—and myself—than I could've imagined. Sandtown's soil had always been mixed that way, holding both struggle and brilliance. And even that soil wasn't new. It was part of the land once walked and worked by the Piscataway, Susquehannock and other native peoples who fished these waters and carved their paths across what we now call Baltimore. Long before I walked those blocks, they had raised Thurgood Marshall, who carried justice from the westside all the way to the United States Supreme Court. Pennsylvania Avenue, just a few steps away, once held the Royal Theatre, where Billie Holiday and Cab Calloway turned pain into sound. By the time I arrived, those lights had dimmed, the theatre was torn down and the headlines about Sandtown told a different story of poverty, crime and decay. Yet as I traversed those same sidewalks, I was still learning about and experiencing life: my first fight, asking a girl for her number, hearing that a friend didn't make it and witnessing police brutality. Sandtown-Winchester is where I watched people nod off on my steps like they were fading in and out of life due to drugs. It's the place where I established lifelong friendships.

Then it was gone – or should I say I was gone from it. My father and his second wife split, and I found myself relocated with Dad to northeast Baltimore. A different world. A new zip code. A place I'd reside for most of my life that never fully replaced what I lost.

With this book, I want to tell a different kind of story about Sandtown—not one soaked in nefarious headlines or crime stats or from the view of a hustler or shooter. This story is told through the eyes of a young Black boy trying to find his way in a world that didn't always move with him. This book is filled with stories that have lingered in my mind for years. In fact, I've spent the last few years reflecting on these stories, wondering how to shape them into something with weight—something readers could sit with and wrestle with. I've come to realize these memories aren't just mine, though. They belong to a lot of us and are the stories of so many Baldamore babies.

Most of my life has unfolded in northeast Baltimore, but west Baltimore, and especially Sandtown, shaped me in ways no zip code can explain. The lessons from those blocks taught me what it means to love your people even when they're struggling. What it means to survive when the system ain't built for you. What it means to find joy anyway—because that joy keeps you going and making even the bleakest days worth living.

These essays are my thank yous. To teachers who saw me. To grandmothers who kept watch. To homies who held me down. To family who stayed close. And to the boy I used to be—the one who didn't know what was coming but walked forward anyway.

Sandtown was a wound and a wellspring, aching and alive with possibility. It shaped me through struggle, grounded me in grit, sustained me through laughter and gave rise to everything I've come to know. And, in many ways, it still does.

I hope these pages do more than tell my truth. I hope they stir something. I hope they make politicians pause and ponder before they pass another policy that impacts 21217. I hope these pages nudge other writers to pick up their pens and deconstruct their pasts. I hope these pages push Baltimoreans to remember how much power we've always had—and still have.

I dare you to look back at the places that made you. To trace the lines between happiness and hardship. To walk back into your past and see the bricks that built you.

Sandtown, thank you.

Thank you for Barbie, Jerome, Melvin, Khalil, Ms. Milam, Ms. Harris, Ciara, Johntay, Li'l Reese, Fat Troy, Black Troy, Andre, Rodney, Chris, Rabbit and so many others—and of course, my father, Albert Phillips Sr., who kept me steady in a place where so many drifted off course.

Now, when people ask me where I'm from, I might still pause out of respect for the many places that hold pieces of me, but I'll always name Sandtown. It is, and will always be, one of the most important places in my story.

These are my truths. These are my tales of Sandtown.

Sincerely,

Albert "L.A." Phillips, Jr.

WHERE YOU FROM?

TALES OF SANDTOWN

TABLE OF CONTENTS

Steps Over West Baltimore, pg 1

A Summer Night in '98, pg 11

Our Pokéman, pg 21

Fat Troy's House Keeps Burning Down, pg 35

Dear Mayor Martin O'Malley, 45

The Tale of Two Cafeterias, pg 53

Concrete Rapunzel, pg 61

The Bake, pg 65

A Lesson Learned, pg 79

We Fit the Description, pg 91

The Final Tale, pg 99

WHERE YOU FROM?

TALES OF SANDTOWN

STEPS OVA WEST BALTIMORE

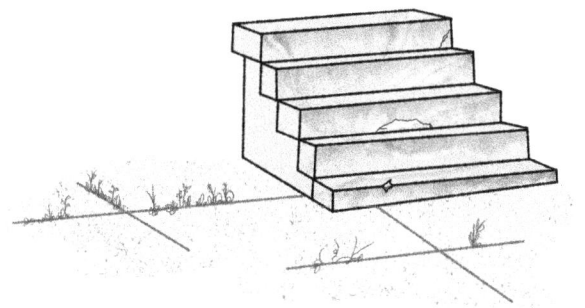

The five, white, marble steps outside my front door were almost always stained with the sticky residue of corner store juices like Huggies and Faygo from the shop at Mosher Street and North Fremont Avenue. Red 40, Blue 1, and Yellow 5 bled together into a messy rainbow that marinated and baked into the stone under the summer heat. That same corner store was where an Asian guy allegedly chopped off his finger while making a customer's sandwich, and where we tossed firecrackers and smoke bombs into the revolving counter before sprinting out, hearts racing faster than our feet.

My stepbrother, Rome was six-foot-something with hazelnut skin, the heartthrob of the neighborhood. He had more women rotating in and out of his upstairs apartment than I can remember. Most importantly to me, he gave me a few dollars nearly every day. I would use his generosity to buy my favorite snacks, Cool Ranch or Nacho Cheese Doritos, a Star Crunch, Andy Capp's Hot Fries and the infamous Blueberry Faygo that made my tongue blue and caused me to burp excessively.

My friends and I would post up on the steps, "making

a mess" as the old heads would say, attracting parades of ants and swarms of bees. Armed with a mop bucket, warm tap water, a scrub brush, Ajax, and plenty of elbow grease, I scrubbed the steps until they gleamed with a pearly white sparkle, fulfilling my father's orders to the letter. A substance abuse counselor who worked just a short drive away, his trips up or down the stairs were always accompanied with a firm and consistent reminder, "LA, scrub these steps before you go anywhere." Obliging his demands, scrubbing became a weekly chore.

I would tell my friends to move, and they would stand or sit on a neighbor's step while I cleaned. I'd start at the top, scrubbing in slow circles, working away dirt, debris, dust and whatever else had settled there, until I reached the bottom step. When I was done, I'd pour the dirty water in the gutter and watch it roll down the street, catching cigarette butts and other things people had discarded before reaching its final destination in the street drain just below the stop sign at the end of the block. Mission accomplished.

My main friends were all guys who lived within a two-block radius of my apartment on North Arlington Avenue. One of my closest friends, Melvin, lived nearby with his elderly parents and curvaceous older sister, Kandy. Like me, he was named after his father. Melvin and I would post up on his steps while playing Pokémon Blue on the Gameboy Colors we got for Christmas. We also both tried our best to manage our Iverson-inspired cornrows in hopes girls would notice. We'd smirk and look at each other when they did.

Body, known by the United States Government as Khalil, lived around the corner on Mosher Street. I couldn't tell you the origin of his nickname, but I can tell you he was usually adorned with a fresh Caesar and the latest Baltimore street wear—an Enyce fit, Nike sneakers and a Nautica jacket, sometimes topped off with a headband to match. He was also known for his button-down shirts that were staunched and ironed just as if he'd gotten them from the cleaners. I don't think his parents lived together, but he split his time between them both. When we weren't playing PlayStation upstairs in his second-floor bedroom, we were on his front steps, using his stereo system to dub our freestyles onto cassette tapes. The raps were about the neighborhood, girls and pseudo-thug stories of work we never moved and guns we never shot. None of our bars was memorable, but the tearful laughs made up for our lack of lyricism.

Next door to me lived Black Troy, who would greet me with a knowing, "You did it again, huh?" every time I misplaced my keys after playing Army Dodgeball in the alley or riding my bike near Dolphin Street. He was a couple of years older, with skin that mirrored Rome's and an athletic build that reminded me of Ricky from Boyz n the Hood, though I don't think he ever played football. I'd take the walk of shame up the narrow stairway to his apartment, and later in the evening, I'd knock on my own door, eyes cast down in embarrassment as my dad or step mom opened it and asked where my key was.

Being a preteen in my neighborhood often meant dealing with peer pressure to have sexual experiences—experiences that were either real or exaggerated but always told in a way to try to make your friends believe them. One time, when my parents weren't home, Black Troy came over and tried to fuck Lacey, a light skinned, neighborhood girl that I'd been crushing on, on my parent's dark grey couch. I opened the front door, and they walked in together. She always wore jean jumpsuits that accentuated her ass, and I couldn't stand seeing him with her. Furious, I kicked them both out and slammed the door like something straight out of an episode of Martin.. The whole thing never put much of a dent in my friendship with Troy; if I got locked out, I'd still end up at his house.

While hanging out when friends and I got too bored, we sometimes annoyed neighborhood drug dealers by yelling out their drug calls from my steps or while lying on the trunks of parked cars.

"Killer bee, killer bee, red tops, red tops," we chanted, until they ice grilled us and told us to knock it off. Secretly, we wanted to be drug dealers. The allure of pockets bulging with money, along with gleaming Mercedes-Benzes and Jaguars made us fascinated by the guys who sold poison to our community. Some of my friends ascended to the occupation, but the thought of calling my father from Central Booking, where my stepmom worked, and saying I was locked up for selling drugs scared me out of considering it a legitimate career choice. That, and the sixty-something-year-old drug addict with the slicked-back ponytail and black cane who used our steps as a Tempur-Pedic mattress, kept me honest. My dad would politely ask her to move whenever she got too comfortable. I would just walk around her and hope she didn't ruin my glistening steps.

These days, twenty-one years removed from North Arlington Avenue, I don't drive through my old neighborhood as often as I once did. At twelve, I left with my dad in the middle of the night, tears running down my face, hitting the steps. The sound of household items crashing and the violent yelling from my father's second divorce still echo in my mind. The old saying about sticks and stones not hurting you was a lie. The bad words kids were told never to say rang out that night like AK-47 bullets, striking their intended targets but wounding me in the crossfire.

The stones saw me at my lowest. In the car, as we pulled away from my neighborhood, my father said something like, "I love you, son. It's going to be alright." I wanted to believe him—I did believe him—but the hurt was still there.

The ghosts of childhood friends lost to gun violence still hover over the neighborhood, begging for remembrance. I heard Li'l Reese, who lived three doors down from me with his older brother, Johntay, was shot to death just a few blocks from his home. He died with dreams unfulfilled. I also heard a childhood friend named Ron—mixed Black and white, light-skinned with curly hair, never fully accepted by either side and always trying to prove himself because of it—jumped off the porch and started pulling his hammer on guys until he was too slow on the draw and lost his life on a concrete battlefield.

Melvin is the only person I know who took five bullets from a Beretta by a guy standing over him—and lived to tell the tale. Bleeding and in shock, he crawled to his house and made it to the hospital. I was among only a few of his homeboys who showed up to his hospital bedside. When we catch up, he still thanks me for it.

Like many impoverished areas of west Baltimore, my old block never evolved. The corner stores, still peddling ultra-processed "foods," never traded them for the organic or gluten-free options that line Whole Foods' shelves. Sadly, the safety and life expectancy of folk living in the Roland Park and Canton neighborhoods never reached our doorsteps.

I still have a few friends from elementary and middle school who remain in the neighborhood, but most traded the disinvested hood for the comforts of suburban homes and gated communities in Baltimore and Howard counties. I can't blame them. As much as the hood shaped me—by giving me my perspective on life, my love for my community and enough memories to last a lifetime—it also handed me far too much pain and turmoil. No one should be forced to wade through poverty and neglect to unearth his or her purpose. However, unfortunately that's the heartbreak, the silent tragedy for so many good souls in the hood.

It's not their personal failing, but rather the merciless, unnatural environment that shaped their lives—the crushing weight of what they were exposed to. The projects are definitely a project, just as the name suggests.

I ain't been in touch with Body since around 2006. Hell, I don't even know if he and Black Troy are still alive. And I went from having sleepovers at Melvin's house in the late 90s to communicating with him only through Facebook when he posts pictures of his sons. Technological advancements, they say.

I once read an article that dated the city's marble steps to the early 1900s, when quarries in Cockeysville supplied the stone that became a symbol of rowhouse pride. I wonder how long the ones I scrubbed have been there and whether a boy like me had scrubbed them before my family's arrival. I'm glad they are marble, though. Cement, wood or metal wouldn't look nearly as pristine. Steps made from those materials wouldn't shine like hood diamonds after a fresh scrub. Ain't no way.

A SUMMER NIGHT IN '98

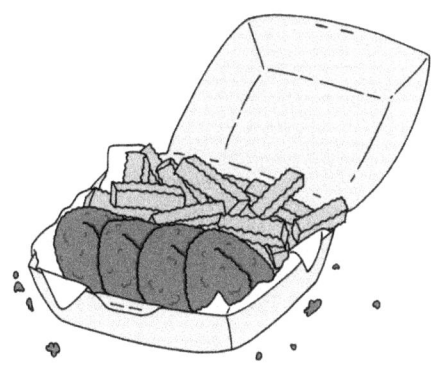

There's nothing more exhilarating and more dangerous than a summer in Baltimore, especially in the trenches.

Trenches (noun): the bottom, the area of the city that's least valued, the place where survival is key, the location where white people are usually cops, coppin' drugs or gentrifying—commonly referred to as the hood.

The Ruff Ryders Anthem defined the summer of 1998. It was platinum on the charts and platinum in the hood—especially in my hood. My brother, Rome, the slickest and most girl-gettingest guy on my street, had it blasting through the movie-theater quality sound system in his apartment, windows wide open, making sure the whole block woke up to it. As I sat on the marble steps outside my house, right below Rome's place, every other car that sped down the 900 block of Arlington Avenue had the track cranked up, the bass hitting so hard it felt like it stomped you in the chest and bare knuckle punched you in the face. It was intense, to say the least.

But it didn't stop there. Cookouts at Druid Hill Park, basketball games at Cloverdale, block parties around the city, barbershops in every hood—hell, anywhere Black people were gathering to vibe—that record had heavy spins. It was the soundtrack of our lives.

More than just a hard-hitting song or a record label, the Ruff Ryders were a movement. Founded by the Dean family from New York and powered by the raw energy of DMX, Eve, The LOX and Swizz Beatz, the collective blended hardcore lyricism with street culture, motorcycles, and pit bulls to create an unmistakable brand. Baltimoreans connected with that energy. The grit of the music felt familiar. The rebellion spoke to a city that has always pushed back, always found a way to survive. Even the Ruff Ryders' pit bull imagery struck a chord. Pit bulls were everywhere in Baltimore, on leashes, stocky and powerful, symbolizing strength, security and aggression. Their music and image defined a generation and became a cultural force that stretched far beyond the music charts.

The hook to Ruff Ryders Anthem was like the national anthem of my neighborhood. It meant to stand on your ten toes. It meant to not accept bullshit from anybody. It meant to consciously live by morals and principles and make others respect you in the process.

At that time, DMX was easily one of my favorite rappers. Baldheaded and rugged, his raw energy was unmatched when it came to music videos, performances and movie roles. He was an urban poet, gifted actor and spiritual teacher trapped in a rapper's body.

I don't remember exactly how I got to watch his breakout movie Belly that year, but I snuck it in somehow—probably at my brother Rome's spot. He was the one who'd let me watch and listen to more explicit music and movies than my parents ever would. I'd sit back and listen as he and his friends debated whether Jay-Z or Nas was more credible in their lyrics.

"Nah, Nas really sold drugs. You can tell by his lyrics. Jay wasn't like that in the streets," Rome said with confidence from his living room sofa.

I hung on every word, getting sworn into the secret society of rap talk. The debates, no matter how heated, always ended rather peacefully. Rome's apartment was right above my parents' place, so it was the perfect escape—a sanctuary from parental rules, an oasis where I could be free and soak up game.

In '98, my birth certificate said I was 8, but my mind felt 15. Also in my mind, I was a grown-ass man handling life like bicycle handlebars, owning its movement with a firm grip.

I still vividly remember being outside way past the time the streetlights came on and coming home to a pissed household. When those lights flickered on, that was the universal alert to shut it down. No pit stops; no store runs no swinging by a friend's house. Just head straight home. No detours. No excuses. Like Monopoly: do not pass Go.

Barbie, my stepmom, with her short Jada Pinkett haircut, gave me the look of disgust only a mother could muster, and my Dad's quiet tension was palpable. In my 8 years, my Dad never whupped me and raised his voice at me only once or twice, so for him to be upset basically meant the end of the world. And Barbie usually lounged on the dark, gray couch in our living room or watched television in my parents' room. But not today. Today, she was right beside my dad, joining in on the scolding.

"LA, where you been at? Why you comin' in so late?" my Dad asked, his tone sharp and serious.

"I was out. Why y'all trippin'? Do I have to report every move I make?" I shot back, like I was a grown man clocking out after a double shift. In my head, all I could hear was the anthem echoing, daring me to stand tall.

Looking back now, I know that's just what 8-year-olds do. At that age, kids are wired to push back, to test how far their independence can stretch. Psychologists might say we're trying to prove we can be trusted, trying to carve out our own little kingdom of control. For me, that meant ignoring curfews at times and imitating rappers who lived by their own rules, even if just for show. At 8, I didn't just want freedom, I wanted control. In my mind, being late wasn't rebellion. It was me being my own boss.

As soon as the words left my mouth, a strange stillness took over me—like the moment just before a glass hits the floor and shatters. I wished I could rewind them like a cassette tape and choose a better response. But life doesn't work that way, and there was no taking them back.

"Yes. Yes, you do, LA." my Dad responded, way calmer than I thought he would. Barbie just shook her head and walked away. My father said a few more words and did the same.

At that moment, I didn't get why they were so concerned, but after a night of reflection across my twin-sized bed, I put the puzzle together. It wasn't complicated, really. They cared about me unconditionally. They just didn't want anything bad to happen to me. And I had plenty of proof to back that up.

I remember Barbie holding my hand tightly in the back of a speeding taxi, racing toward Johns Hopkins Hospital. I could barely breathe, wheezing from a chronic asthma attack, struggling just to speak in broken sentences. But Barbie was right there beside me, comforting me with the instinctive care that moms provide.

I remember my Dad stepping up a year ago, taking on the responsibility of raising me when my biological mom, battling mental health struggles, couldn't. He became the man I needed, choosing to raise me in a city where fatherless homes were far too common.

Their care for me was written all over their actions. They didn't want me to become another statistic, one of thousands of people of color who go missing – or get killed – every year.

I respected it, but part of me still felt like I was in the right. I mean, I made it home in one piece. Wasn't that enough?

I didn't elaborate to my parents, but I know exactly why I didn't come in on time. I was out frolicking around the block, chillin' with my friends not even thinking about being in the house on a vibrant summer night. Why would I want to be home on time? That was the opposite of how Ruff Ryders rolled.

Lames went in on time. Clowns went in on time. Children went in on time. I didn't see myself as lame, a clown or a child (though clearly biologically I was), so that's why coming in on time didn't matter to me. I imagined DMX probably didn't get home on time either when his parents were expecting him to. I wanted to be the same way. I muttered those thoughts to myself, lying in my dark room, staring at the ceiling. The internal battle between my real 8-year-old self and the imagined 15- and 30-something versions of me raged on, each trying to justify my actions. I juggled these thoughts as I drifted into slumber.

The next day, Melvin came knocking on my door, with my boy, Body, right behind him. Body lived around the corner in the middle of Mosher Street, but everyone on my block knew him. And everybody on his block knew me and Melvin, too. We were so tight, people probably thought we were family. They were my brothers, my best friends.

They were out recruiting boys from around the way to play Army Dodgeball. The game was simple, but with an imaginary, more brutal twist. Regular dodgeball had the usual rules—get hit, you're out. But in Army Dodgeball, you could keep playing unless you were hit in both legs, the head or your torso. So, if someone pegged you in the left leg, you had to keep playing, hopping around on your right leg. It was a whole new level of competitiveness.

We played until the sun dipped, and the streetlights flickered on. That's when we saw a few girls from our elementary school walking by. I locked eyes with Lacy, a fifth grader who was straight-up a goddess in my eyes. Her caramel skin and eyes that seemed to call my name made my heart race. She was my Jet magazine page 43 "Beauty of the Week."

While walking and flirting with our school crushes, we ended up near my house. I had to make a quick decision.

- Option 1: Go inside and be responsible.
- Option 2: Stay outside and show Lacy I was the 8-year-old man she needed in her life.

Easily swayed by the allure of Lacy, I chose the latter, ignoring the streetlights' silent plea to come home.

After another hour of flirting the best way an 8-year-old knew how, I dapped up the homies, told Lacy I'd be back for her love and finally went inside. As soon as I did, all of my nighttime excitement was extinguished by the look of two disappointed parents. As they questioned my whereabouts and actions, again, I heard the anthem echoing in my mind, convincing me I was doing only what we all believed in.

Even now, whenever I hear that beat drop, I don't

just think about DMX or Ruff Ryders. I remember the 8-year-old boy with cornrows, chubby cheeks and a block head, sitting on marble steps, reaching for a sense of manhood bigger than him. DMX had grown men barking and gritting their teeth like pit bulls, and to me, that was power, that was command. And when I hear it today, I don't just hear the music. I also hear that boy inside me, still chasing the rhythm telling him to stand tall, still wrestling with a world that doesn't make space for softness, still learning, after all these years, how to be his own boss.

OUR POKÉMON

Secretly, every child in my hood wished he or she had a superpower like Marvel or DC Comic heroes and villains. Invisibility, invincibility, teleportation, super strength or just to be ridiculously wealthy like Bruce Wayne or Tony Stark — any of those supernatural abilities would suffice.

Unfortunately, our imaginations never manifested our most sought after superpowers, so in 1999, we settled for Pokémon to fill some of the void. I have no clue where Pokémon came from. I mean, I know it was created in Japan, but kids like me had no idea how the hell it made it 6,776 miles all the way from Japan to our west Baltimore television screens.

A few weeks before the Christmas of '99, my dad gave me a brochure listing toys being released just in time for the big day. Companies mastered their timing of putting out these toy guides, getting them into the hands of kids like us. Mongoose bikes, PlayStation games, remote-controlled cars and others were all listed with bright colors and bold letters.

"Just mark what you want and hand it back when you're done," Dad said, handing the brochure to me, before heading out the door to work. His long shifts as a substance abuse counselor meant the refrigerator door was always home to a list of chores waiting for me—tasks to fill the hours between jamming my thumbs into video game controllers and roaming the streets. Dad didn't always give me everything I wanted—like the sunglasses I threw a fit over when he refused to buy them at the mall one time—but he made sure I had most things. I figured his gold chains and rings meant he always had money, even if he didn't. Plus, at age nine, I couldn't have cared less about a budget.

I quickly devoured my bowl of Peanut Butter Cap'N Crunch and proceeded to complete the mission my father bestowed upon me. Not the chores but the Christmas gift selections. Pen in hand, I marked most of the first page. Then, I marked most of the second page. After a little mental reevaluation, I went back and marked all of the first page. Then, I marked two more toys on the second page. Within 15 minutes, I had 97 percent of the brochure marked with circles and check marks. Circles meant I really wanted it. Check marks meant I really, really, really wanted it. A Gameboy Color and the Pokémon Blue game were at the top of my list. When I finished treating the pamphlet like a Bingo sheet, I sat it on my Dad and stepmom's bed and walked outside to see who was on the block.

"Peanut, what your dumb ass doin' on my block? I told you this my territory, li'l boy," I yelled to the corner of Arlington and Mosher where Peanut was crossing the street. Peanut's head was literally shaped like a peanut with the indentation and all. I think it came from playing tackle football in the alley and having his head dribble off the pavement too many times.

"Whatever, I run this side just like I run my side!" he yelled back. Peanut lived around the corner on Pennsylvania Avenue near Shake N Bake. It was literally a few minutes away, but I always made it known that he wasn't in his hood when he stepped on my block. It was our special way of greeting each other.

"Where you headed to?" I asked him, as I walked closer to meet him.

"The Avenue Market. Walk up there with me, yo. I'm about to grab some Pokémon cards."

The Avenue Market was the only store in my neighborhood that sold Pokémon cards. From Charizard and Blastoise to Mewtwo and Pikachu, they had nearly all the most popular cards — all the cards kids like us wanted due to seeing them on television.

"Let me get the three decks right there," Peanut told the Asian man behind the counter, pointing at the decks through the class container.

Kids like us were regulars in the store, but the Asians still treated us like we were serial bank robbers. Their slow steps followed us down every aisle, their narrowed eyes tracking every item our hands grazed. It wasn't just suspicion—it was a quiet, practiced hostility, the kind Harvard professor Chester Pierce would define as a microaggression. Other times, they didn't even bother with subtlety, accusing us of breaking some unwritten rule, like speaking at a decibel level they deemed too loud, and shooed us from their storefront back into the open market space. Today they were oddly chill, though.

"If you getting those, I'm going to get the one over here," I said, while staring a fully evolved Charizard card in the face with eyes bursting with excitement.

When you went to K-Mart or one of the higher-end stores, your cards were hidden in a fancy, polypropylene package, similar to potato chip bags. But when you went to the spots in the trenches to grab your decks, they were in Ziploc style plastic bags like sandwiches.

This cheaper style packaging from hood stores was accompanied by fake cards. You knew they were fake because when you held them up to the sunlight, you could see straight through them. Also, the colors were faded like they were printed on a home printer instead of factory machinery. Most kids in the hood wouldn't bother you too much about it, but the kids who purchased only the authentic cards would call you poor if you pulled them out.

As we walked back toward my apartment, we littered the sidewalk with the bags previously housing our cards.

"Let me see your cards, Peanut. You got some good ones?"

"Not really," he replied in the saddest voice I ever heard him respond.

Lured like kids to the sound of an ice cream truck, we were intrigued by the first card we saw in the pack. We judged a book by its cover, disregarding what the elders had taught us. We were stuck with one or two notable cards and a bunch of other unknown and weaker ones. The television show's theme song taught us to "catch' em all," but we didn't want these phony ass cards.

Still, we proceeded to battle.

Pokémon had no rule book that made it to 21217. It didn't travel 6,776 miles like the television show. We just made shit up.

A few minutes into walking up Fremont Avenue, I found my first challenger.

"Hol' up. Hol' up. Hol' up. That Bulbasaur ain't fuckin' with this Golbat," I yelled to make sure the conviction in my voice translated to agreement from the small, onlooking crowd.

Hood Pokémon Rule #1: If you yelled something with enough conviction, and people bought it, you won the round. If they didn't, they'd clown you hard, questioning your entire grasp of Pokémon—the game none of us really knew how to play anyway.

Pokémon was so popular back then that random kids from the neighborhood would gather around, watching us play while trying desperately to decode the rules—rules that were nonexistent.

"You ain't gon' beat Man Man, yo. He got all the

good cards cause his mom buys them from official card dealers and shit like that," Peanut told me, as we trekked to Man Man's hood on Riggs Avenue to see who the hood Pokémon champion of the world was.

Before we got to his front door, we saw Man Man's little brother, Jason, outside on his red Big Wheel that was too small for his long legs that hit his elbows when he rode it.

"Tell Man Man come outside now and bring his cards," I told Jason, like we were about to square up on the yellow lines in the middle of the street.

On the surface, I was as steady as a brick wall, but inside, my heart thundered like the pounding bass drums of a marching band. I could either become a legend or become a clown depending on how this battle went.

Before Jason could tell me Man Man wasn't in the house, I heard his voice about ten feet behind me. Man Man was taller than most boys our age, and his voice carried a depth beyond its years. For a moment, I thought it was a teenager calling out to me.

"What y'all doing on my block? This ain't Arlington or Pennsylvania avenues," he said, while stopping and looking at us with stern eyes that refused to blink.

He had a crew of guys from his block with him, and just like that, it turned into a standoff. It felt like the Wild West or a Bloods versus Crips showdown—eyes locked, faces hardened, and my Pokémon deck gripped in my hand like a loaded pistol.

"I heard you was that guy on the Pokémon tip. I'm tryin' to see what the talk is about. Let's battle," I told him.

Ready for battle, he quickly tossed his plastic bag full of Nacho Cheese Sunflower seeds and and Blue Ranch Doritos to his entourage and pulled his cards out of his left, back pocket like a Crip flag.

"You ain't said nothing but a word. Let's get it."

I started the battle with the fully evolved Charizard that attracted me to the counterfeit deck in the first place, mainly because I knew it was the best card I had. It also helped me win a battle before getting to Man Man.

"That's cute. I'm about to fuck you up. I want you to remember that you asked for this, not me," Man Man said, a moment before pulling out a holographic Blastoise card.

Hood Pokémon Rule #2: Blastoise was a powerful water Pokémon. Charizard was a fearsome fire Pokémon. One rule we did follow was the rule of elements: Fire usually beats grass, water beats fire, and electric Pokémon—like Ash's Pikachu—could fry most water types since water conducts electricity. I guess William Pinderhughes Elementary taught us something useful after all. Water douses fire, so I lost that round without a fight.

From the corner of my eye, I saw Peanut shake his head and look up to the sky like he was asking Jesus to pick my next card for me.

"You got me. You got me. But I ain't done yet—I got something for your ass," I said, my confidence shaky, knowing full well I didn't have a damn thing for him. By then, the heat from my body was battling the cold winter air. My rising temperature, mixed with nerves, turned my underarms into puddles. I began to stretch my arms a little farther from my torso, trying to avoid the sensation of soaking wetness under my GAP hoodie.

He started the next round with an Electrobuzz, an electric Pokémon with Black stripes and fanged teeth.

Peanut, giving me hints, balled his right fist and stared at me while tapping it with his left index finger. After a few moments of struggling to translate his message, his clue finally hit me. He was telling me to play a rock-style Pokémon because they were stronger against electric-style Pokémons. I remember watching that play out on the television show, too. Pikachu kept trying to electrocute a rock Pokémon, and he eventually lost and realized he should have used a different move.

Realizing I had the upper hand, I smirked at Peanut and said, "Try your luck against my Onix." Onix was a long, snake-looking Pokémon with a body made of boulders and a head with a horn at the top.

The eyes of some guys of Man Man's s crew got bigger as he whispered in another guy's ear. I knew they knew I had easily won this round.

"Okay, you got this one. I ain't gon' lie. I wasn't expecting that," said Man Man, as he nodded his head confirming my victory.

By this time, a number of people surrounded us watching the duel. Kids our age, dope fiends, two people in wheelchairs, a car full of police officers and a bunch of other people all hoovered around us trying to see who the victor would be. We were a hood spectacle.

"For this final round, I got something special for you. I was saving the best for last," said Man Man, while grinning from ear to ear.

Still sweating like a snitch, I yelled, "Just put your card out!"

In the blink of an eye, a Mewtwo card jumped into the battle. This card was considered the best card in all of Pokémon. I never saw one in real life, but on the video game and television show, nobody was fucking with Mewtwo. He was like the Pokémon God.

Peanut started doing the Father, Son and Holy Spirit prayer with his right index finger like Catholics do. He didn't even go to church, but this battle had him elbow deep in his religious bag. I guess he thought I needed some form of higher power to save me from this last round.

He was right.

Looking through my cards, I couldn't find anything that came nearly close to the level of Mewtwo. I knew I was going to lose regardless of what I put out, but at least I could give the spectators a good laugh before my reputation was ruined.

In the voice of a trained actor, I told Man Man he was in for something epic. Then, I reached into my deck and pulled out the lamest card known to the Pokémon world.

"Nigga, did you just put out a Jigglypuff? I know you ain't just put out a Jigglypuff. What the fuck?!" Peanut said, before anyone else could respond.

The whole crowd around us busted out laughing and quickly began to disperse. The wheelchairs rolled away, the police cars sped off and the dope fiends went to chase their next high.

"See, I don't know why you came around here looking for me. I do this Pokémon shit in my sleep. Take your ass back to Arlington Avenue somewhere," said Man Man, before bursting out laughing and dapping up me and Peanut.

I took my defeat like a champ, but while walking back home, all I could think of was how the battle would have gone if I had a better deck, but one loss and one win ain't a bad record.

"Jigglypuff. Yo' you bold for playing that card in the hood. You deserve an award for that. It should say 'this award is presented to the first person to play a Jigglypuff card in the hood' or something like that," Peanut said before dapping me up and heading back to his block.

When I got back home, the streetlights had just come on and my Dad was in the house watching TV.

Before I could say anything, he used the remote to mute the sound and said, "You must think I'm rich or something."

FAT TROY'S HOUSE KEEPS BURNING DOWN

Most days after school were spent doing homework on fractions, watching Cartoon Network reruns, riding my black Huffy with its slow-leaking back tire or screaming at the 32-inch television while playing PlayStation.

While scrolling channels, knowing I would inevitably end up watching Dragon Ball Z, I managed to land on the news. The news always felt relentlessly grim, dominated by reports of violence, and today was no exception. On Edmondson Avenue, a man was murdered. Shortly after, another shooting claimed a life near Belair Road. As if that wasn't enough, yet another killing occurred just minutes from my elementary school on Calhoun Street. Three shootings. Three lives lost. Zero witnesses.

As disheartening as the killings were, the worst news I saw on my television screen was the house of my friend, Fat Troy, burning down. Everybody called him Fat Troy to create a distinction from Black Troy, who lived right next door to me, and because, well, he was fat. Proximity and mutual interests made Fat Troy and I friends. We played video games together after school and on the weekends. He didn't have many video games, so I would usually bring my game systems and video games to his house for our classic showdowns of Pokémon and NBA Live. I'd win at most of the games I brought over; he'd claim victory on the ones he already had.

But on this day, I watched in horror as I witnessed his home being engulfed by flames. My heart pounded noticeably louder and my breaths were like those of a marathon finisher as I thought about what this could mean for Fat Troy and his family.

"Oh shit, Fat Troy's house is on fire," I said to myself, flinging open my front door. I spent a few frantic seconds unlocking the vestibule door to the building, then jumped down the front steps, clearing them in a single leap. My feet hit the pavement hard as I stopped to take in what I was witnessing.

Fat Troy lived just a stone's throw away on the other side of Mosher Street, next to a large alleyway.

As I sprinted toward his residence, I smelled the pungent odor of smoke and saw the massive blaze engulfing the place Fat Troy once called home. Luminous yellow and orange flames danced, their heat licking the air as the wood crackled like a colossal campfire. The inferno swelled, raising the temperature of the entire block like a fierce sun of destruction.

Firefighters were on the scene, and the same news reporter I saw on my living room television screen was now in front of me with a large crowd surrounding her. Her generic voice barely contained g the concern I had for the moment. I saw some of my closest comrades, too—Ron, Melvin, Body, Black Troy and Bradley—viewing the mayhem from the other side of the street. They were posturing the way we all did in moments of calamity—hiding tears, cracking jokes, saying little that stirred emotion yet full of endless, disturbing thoughts.

It felt like we were witnessing our friend and his family being burned alive, their bodies consumed by fire, their spirits rising with the smoke into the afternoon sky. I couldn't tell if what I saw in my mind was real—or just my fear taking shape.

I had only one question, but I was scared to ask it. The answer I didn't want might give me dreams I couldn't get rid of. After taking a breath as deep as my lungs could manage, I mustered the confidence to inquire about Fat Troy's wellbeing.

"Anybody seen them get out?" I asked the large crowd, my voice brittle with worry. Concern coiled around my words, tight and suffocating, like a snake around its prey. Fortunately, it seemed I was the only uninformed person there.

An older woman in the neighborhood, with her hair tied in a red bandana and a burning cigarette hanging from her mouth, let me know Troy and his family had recently moved out. I wondered why I didn't know – how I lost contact, how I became unaware. Nonetheless, I was certainly glad Fat Troy was not roasting along with his residence.

Troy's house was simultaneously a safe haven and arcade. Out front were marble steps like mine, like most others in the neighborhood. Inside, we never sat at the small, circular, wooden table in the kitchen or the worn, brown couch that fashioned the living room. We always walked briskly to his room, the one he shared with his younger, skinnier brother, DJ. The carpet was dark blue, stale and dusty from years of tracked-in shoe prints, and the metal bunk bed where we sat was probably the sturdiest piece of furniture in the whole house. None of the fixtures or features mattered much to me, or to our bond as friends—brothers, really. What stayed with me was Troy's matted miniature afro, always in need of a fresh trim and lineup, and his chubby, brown cheeks—the color of warm cinnamon rolls fresh out the oven.

No danger ever emanated from Troy's house. No fear. No yelling. None of the domestic squabbles that echoed through so many homes like ours. In fact, I can barely remember ever seeing his parents. The place felt quiet, like it existed on the edge of the noise, though it was fully within it.

The word on the street was the cause of the fire was a mystery. I was a believer in many things as a child –maybe pro wrestling being real, but not in flames magically appearing in houses.

I asked my friends if anyone knew where Troy had moved, if he had a number I could dial. No one had an answer. He wasn't in my grade at school, and he was absent more often than most, so I didn't think much of it when I didn't see him for stretches of time. That was just how things were back then—some kids were around one week and gone the next. We didn't talk every day, not because of any fallout but instead because of the kind of preteen lives we lived. He might be visiting family out of town, and I'd be across the city at a cousin's house. Still, standing just a few steps away from the frenzy, I found myself wondering if I was the kind of friend I thought I was. The kind of friend I meant to be.

Months later, history repeated itself. Fat Troy's house was bursting in flames again, but there were no news cameras this time. The crowd also wasn't as thick. There were just the unmistakable sirens of fire trucks pulling up through the wide street and alley near his house.

This time, we knew why the house burned down. The streets talked again. They said vacant homes in the hood meant a few things. They were either dope-fiend gathering places or empty playhouses for kids to roam free and fuck shit up with no repercussions from adults. The latter got me and my cousins a whupping from my grandmother when she lived on Orleans Street. They went inside a vacant house, one Granny had told us never to set foot in. I watched and didn't stop them. We all got every lick Granny's leather belt offered. God rest her soul.

Anyway, one of these two groups set fire to Fat Troy's house the second time. Just like with the murders on the news, though, there were zero witnesses. Unfortunately, the concern was not as palpable as the first fire. It felt like worry had packed up and wandered out of Sandtown.

Fat Troy's house, like so many others in Sandtown, was just another structure at risk—whether from vicious fires, unwarranted violence or time itself. The flames that consumed it weren't just destroying a home; they were feeding on a city already burning with neglect.

In January 2022, Baltimore City had 15,032 vacant homes. Fifteen thousand thirty-two roofs that could shelter families. Fifteen thousand, thirty-two buildings with walls that could shield the homeless from the bitter bite of winter nights. Instead, these homes sat silent, rotting. They're not just empty—they're abandoned hopes, breeding grounds for trouble, for cat-sized rats. For despair. In some neighborhoods, block after block is a graveyard of hollow houses, where the living are outnumbered by ghosts. These homes aren't just wasting space—they're tangible reminders of abandonment and the heartbreaking acceptance of deterioration.

I rode by Troy's house a few years ago during my lunch break from my job at the Baltimore City Public Schools' district office. I got out of my car and stood in front of the steps for a few minutes. Time froze and I was back sitting on the bottom of his bunk bed, annihilating him in whatever game he took out of my FuncoLand storage bag. The serenity wrapped in that moment made me smile a bit. I stood there for a few seconds taking it all in.

The neighbors probably thought I was an investor or undercover police officer due to my business casual attire. Little do they know, I just wanted to see if Fat Troy's house had burned down again. I was curious about the conditions of my old street, of North Arlington Avenue, of my stomping grounds.

Fortunately, the neighborhood was rehabbed, and a new family was living in the home. Their curtains hung in the windows and the sound from a television could be heard from where I stood. Grey and grainy steps were there now instead of the marble ones, and the door was covered in dark blue paint. All seemed well. Even if the house had burned to the ground, leaving nothing but weightless ashes, the memories of our bond would remain—like coals that burn hot but never disintegrate, steady and unextinguished.

DEAR MAYOR MARTIN O'MALLEY

"Class, today we are writing letters to the most notable elected official in Baltimore City, Mayor Martin O'Malley. Your letter needs to be error free and written in the friendly letter format we have been practicing all week," Ms. Milam announced to the fourth grade class on a Thursday morning at William Pinderhughes Elementary.

Ms. Milam was the strictest teacher to ever teach at the school, according to every student who was ever taught by her. She made up for her five-foot-three-inch stature with a Shaquille O'Neal-like presence. Her smiles were few and far between; her grim look almost felt permanently placed with a Sharpie.

If you attempted to turn the class into Def Comedy Jam, you could expect her to get the last laugh by calling your parents immediately after school. If you forgot the chronological order of U.S. presidents while you were standing in front of the class reciting them, she would spare no embarrassment and would Magic Johnson, no-look-pass point you to your assigned seat. There were rarely any warnings from her. She had no time for them.

Although she was stern, I sort of liked her because I knew she cared. Her draconian nature led to extra attention that wasn't provided by many other teachers. Her eyes saw virtually everything, and her ears heard everything her eyes didn't catch. The hyperfocus she had on her students made me feel seen at all times, even when I was avoiding her surveillance.

The night before we were to write letters to the mayor, like some nights before that, I struggled to sleep. The sounds of a rustling metal gate and constant footsteps outside my first-floor, alley-adjacent window kept me awake. The regular assembly line of people going in and out of 919 N. Arlington Ave — a vacant house next door to me — annoyed and intrigued me while keeping me from my needed school-night slumber. Some nights, I'd peek out my white, vinyl blinds to see people rush in and out of the abandoned house like a Kmart Superstore. They all had eyes that looked far too alert for nighttime, regardless of whether they were coming or going. I heard from old heads that's what being high and wanting to be high did to you. They looked like they needed something more — rehab, God or a combination of the two.

"Ms. Milam, can we write about whatever we want?" I asked, wondering if my stories of sleepless nights and dope fiends could make it from my brain onto paper and into an envelope to be given to Mayor O'Malley.

"Yes, whatever you want, but please make sure it's school appropriate," she responded.

Remembering the friendly letter format Ms. Milam

ingrained in our hippocampus that week, I started my letter with a heading before addressing the recipient, the mayor.

Next, it was time to get into the heart of the letter.

"Dear Mayor Martin O'Malley:" is how we were all made to start our letters. Ms. Milam wrote it on the board since students kept forgetting how to spell the mayor's last name.

"Sometimes I can't sleep at night because junkies are constantly going in and out of the vacant house next door to mine. My room is on the first floor near the alley, so sometimes I think about one of them climbing in my window."

I wrote two or three more paragraphs detailing my situation before pleading with the mayor to act.

"In conclusion, I want you to rebuild the vacant home into a home where somebody lives, so the junkies won't be using it as a drug house. That way, I can get more sleep at night and not be tired in school. Thank you.

Sincerely,

Albert Phillips Jr."

I turned in my paper that day, excited to know the mayor would soon read my letter and be called to act swiftly. When he was interviewed on the news, he seemed to care about everyone. He was always holding press conferences about crime and other issues in the city, so I looked forward to how he would respond to my request. I was also excited Ms. Milam made me correct only a few errors, which means I did a good job with the writing.

One week later, as class was being dismissed, I pulled Ms. Milam to the side and asked her if Mayor O'Malley had written back to me. I wanted to know what his elaborate plan was and if he needed my help in figuring out where to start. I had no knowledge of demolition or renovation, but I figured I might be able to give him a pointer or two.

But before I could share my plan, Ms. Milam abruptly cut me off and said, "I'm sorry, Mr. Phillips. He has not replied yet. Once I hear something, I will let you know."

I thanked her for the update and walked home wondering why the mayor's response was taking so long. Did he not care about what I had to say? Was I not convincing enough? Is he scared to come to the hood?

A year later, my fifth-grade year came to a close with still no word from our mayor, the same mayor who still found time for press conferences and other TV appearances. He found time to talk to reporters, radio hosts and other concerned residents — everyone except me, it seemed. For over a year, whenever I saw him on TV, I would quickly change the channel or turn it off. He was the mayor, but he wasn't my mayor.

The next school year, I entered middle school at Furman L. Templeton.

A few months into the school year, my class was called to take a field trip to the corner of Pennsylvania Avenue and Dolphin Street. Baltimore's busiest mayor was there greeting his constituents and taking pictures with everyone in sight. With the thought of him ignoring my letter in mind, I had no interest in meeting him. I didn't want to shake his hand and thank him for his service. I wasn't interested in being in his next campaign commercial or telling my family he graced me with his presence.

"Class, let's line up and head to see the mayor across the street. You can leave your belongings in the classroom since we will be returning in about 30 minutes," announced Ms. Wilson, my sixth grade ELA teacher, who had no clue I was mentally beefin' with the white mayor she was ushering the class to greet him and pose for a picture.

As we took the short stroll, I thought back to the resentment I felt over not getting a reply from the city's leader when I was in the fourth grade. My heart fluttered from a nervous anger and my breaths deepened like I was doing meditation. Smiling with the artificial smile all politicians had mastered while talking to neighborhood folks, the mayor, wearing a dark-blue suit, eventually greeted my class. Many of my friends showed nearly all 32 teeth in a zombie-like trance as they lined up to shake his hand, but I refused to wear the mask. My enraged spirit was torn between telling him exactly how I felt and delivering him a right hook like Mike Tyson often used to punish opponents.

I decided neither was appropriate and one could land me in handcuffs, so I drifted to the back of the bunch and stewed in my feelings.

"Come on class, it's time to take a picture before we head back in the building," said Ms. Wilson as she herded all students in position to be on camera. I can't remember if I faked a smile or not, but I hope I didn't. I hope I maintained the fire that started in fourth grade and continued to sixth grade. I hope my temperament made the mayor feel uncomfortable in my presence. I hope he whispered to Ms. Wilson, "Is he okay?" while noticing my displeased disposition, as I stood off at a distance. I hope I caused him to feel some fear.

Though I had no evidence the mayor received and read my letter, I also had no evidence he didn't, so that was enough to self-justify my disregard for him. It was enough for me to believe when my Dad would say things like, "All politicians do is lie, get voted in and then keep lying." Plus, I don't think any of my classmates ever heard from him either.

Around March 2002, the booming trap house was renovated by the property owner. It sounded like the construction workers pounded at least 10,000 nails into different parts of the house, and the grass was trimmed up nicely, too. As the flowers bloomed and the crisp spring air brought a renewed feeling, the nighttime annoyance was replaced with a family of renters. The nightly noises ceased, and my nights of REM sleep increased.

Thanks for nothing, Mayor Martin O'Malley.

THE TALE OF TWO CAFETERIAS

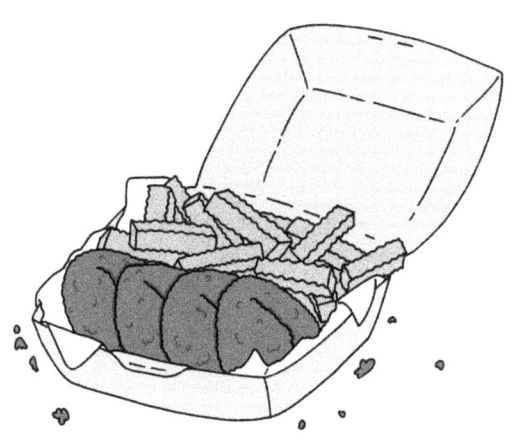

"You don't even have to ask me that dumb question! You already know how I like my chicken boxes. I've been coming here since I was a little girl. I want salt, pepper, ketchup and hot sauce all over," Ms. Patty shouted while glaring at Mr. Lee, after he dared to ask her what condiments she wanted on her order. As she yelled, her face screwed up like a down-south mixtape.

Ms. Patty fussed even when they got her food right. Most days, she was about an eight on the "I'm-about-to-go-off-on-somebody" scale, so most people kept their conversations with her short and sweet, trying to avoid igniting her temper and feeling her wrath.

He must have lost his damn mind asking me what I want on my chicken box like I ain't spent my life's fortune at this food stall, she muttered aloud, letting the words drift through the air as the crowd in the Avenue Market buzzed around her. The market sat across the street from my third elementary school, William Pinderhughes, so I'd witnessed this scene, which my eyes followed like miniature news cameras as I laughed to myself, countless times.

Some mornings, before my Dad dropped me off at

school, we'd swing by the Avenue Market to grab breakfast sandwiches. The smell of frying eggs and sizzling bacon filled the atmosphere like clouds as people bustled in and out.

Before you even pushed open the double doors, which were badly in need of a fresh coat of paint, you were hit with the harsh greeting of stale cigarette smoke and the sour stench of piss—probably from a feen who had urinated on the wall outside the door again. It happened so often I wondered why there weren't Porta Potties outside.

I usually ordered the same thing from the same spot, with the same familiar faces behind the counter. In the hood, we remember faces quicker than names, and everyone gets a nickname. If you had a scar on your face, you were Scarface. If your breath smelled like death, you were Funk Breath. If your grandmother had a mustache thicker than most of the men in the neighborhood, she was Man Face. It wasn't personal (most of the time); it's just how we remembered people.

My friends and family called me LA (Little Albert) since I was a junior, but the people from around the way who didn't know me probably called me something else. Given the size of my dome, I'm pretty sure I was referred to as "big head li'l boy" more than once or twice.

After Ms. Patty stormed out, I walked to the counter and glanced at the menu I'd memorized years earlier. I ordered my usual bacon, egg and cheese sandwich with butter and jelly on toasted white bread. If my ribs were touching, I'd get two, but one was enough today. That bowl of Cap'n Crunch I had before leaving the house had already put a dent in my appetite.

My Dad ordered the same thing, like clockwork, and didn't even have to think about it. Like me, he was a creature of habit when it came to breakfast.

After we grabbed our morning grub, we hopped into my Dad's Ford Expedition and he drove me to school. The scent of bacon and eggs lingered in the air, rising from the brown paper bags and the warm parchment paper cradling our sandwiches. They were cut diagonally—just the way I liked it. The sweet grape jelly balanced the salty bacon, and together they transformed the yellow eggs, swaddled in melted American cheese, into something greater than the sum of their parts. I chewed slowly and purposefully, savoring each bite.

As we cruised, the sounds of Neo Soul legends like Maxwell and Erykah Badu blasted through the subwoofers while my Dad's work badges dangled from the rearview mirror. The sounds became a melody to my feast. I finished my sandwich as we parked in front of the school. Then I dapped him up and headed inside, full and ready to take on the day.

It was May, which meant testing season. Scantrons and number two pencils were everywhere, and teachers throughout the building were constantly saying, "Stop talking" and "Raise your head up from your desk." Teachers pushed us to the brink of self-destruction. And when our pencils broke and the classroom sharpener was missing or busted, Mr. Cooper, an administrator with a perfectly shaped afro who held it down in the front office, sharpened them with his thumbnail – a skill that baffles me to this day.

By the time lunch rolled around four, long hours later, the school's idea of a meal awaited us. The menu featured an unidentifiable meat slathered in barbecue sauce, a carton of white, chocolate or strawberry milk, unseasoned string beans, mashed potatoes that stuck to the roof of your mouth and a piece of fruit that was about as appetizing as a brick. The "food" was mostly pre-packaged, with not an ounce of soul or care put into any of it. We joked it was prison food. We still ate it though—or used it as ammunition during our food fights.

The lunch ladies rushed us through the line, eyes sharp like ATF agents, ensuring we weren't sneaking anything extra. Honestly, nobody ever really wanted extra unless they were serving chicken nuggets or pizza. Even the kids with less food at home wouldn't dare go back for seconds—not in front of their friends, anyway. There was pride in accepting only what you were given, no matter how appetizing it was.

I thought all school lunches were like mine—mystery meat and Cloverland milk seemed like staples in every cafeteria. Before William Pinderhughes, I went to Hilton Elementary and Mildred D. Monroe Elementary, and the menu was always the same. A year later, I attended Furman L. Templeton for sixth grade and, lo and behold, the lunch followed me there. The only difference was the ladies serving it.

Things changed near the end of my sixth-grade year when I visited The Park School of Baltimore, a private school twenty minutes from mine. My Dad and my sixth-grade English teacher, Ms. Wilson, who introduced me to mozzarella sticks, were helping me find a better middle school since my current one wasn't approved for seventh and eighth grade by Baltimore City Public Schools.

Walking into The Park School felt like stepping into an entirely different world. The first thing I noticed were the ducks happily frolicking on the freshly trimmed, green grass. Until then, I thought ducks hung out at only the Inner Harbor. As we entered the building, students walked with purpose to their classes, their strides more deliberate, as though they were eager to be there. And when we stepped into classrooms, students' eyes were fixed on the teacher, their ears clinging to every word. At this school, I couldn't imagine an argument, let alone a fight.

My Dad and Ms. Wilson were there to talk academics, questioning the administration about test scores, scholarships and grade point averages. I was there just to scope out the cafeteria, which was only a short walk from the classroom I was in.

It smelled like it was filled with love, and it probably was. One of the cafeteria workers was outside grilling chicken on an actual grill, not pulling it from a huge metal pan of water like at my school. Kids casually went back for seconds—some even thirds. The options were endless. Fresh salads, ripe fruit, grilled chicken and freshly cooked vegetables. They also had a breakfast station where you could make your own waffles. It was like their cafeteria was sponsored by Golden Corral!

At one point, my dad went to meet with members of the administration in an office while I shadowed one of the few Black boys I remember seeing at the school. Outside of the Disney Channel, I had never seen so many young white kids in one place in my life. I wondered how he felt being one of the only Black boys at the school, but I kept my thoughts about race relations to myself and never asked him.

Carlton from *The Fresh Prince of Bel-Air* was the only person I could think of that mirrored the boy— not much in appearance but in demeanor. He was quirky and extra happy, which struck me as kind of odd. It was like he was programmed that way or something. It just didn't feel natural.

"Here's the... and that's the... and we won this award for..." I drowned out all of his words, which to me felt soulless and scripted.

After the tour, I thought about dapping up the "Carlton" boy, but opted for a nice, formal handshake instead. I figured he'd prefer that anyway.

Something about the whole experience made me feel out of place. Maybe it was the artificial welcome of "Carlton," the manufactured smiles of the staff I met or just the uneasiness from being out of west Baltimore, out of my comfort zone.

I don't remember telling my Dad I didn't want to attend The Park School, but he vividly recalls me saying I didn't like it, so he decided to look elsewhere. He ended up landing on St. Anthony of Padua, a Catholic school in northeast Baltimore.

Looking back, I probably didn't believe I was worthy of such an institution. Internalized oppression? Imposter Syndrome? In need of more Black folk? Maybe it was a combination of all three.

Nonetheless, I will never forget the alluring scent of that cafeteria. It had me in a trance. That day, I realized the tale of two cafeterias. Mystery meat versus tender, sliced chicken, bright red apples versus dull pears, white bread versus wheat bread with the little oat pieces. My eyes witnessed it; my tastebuds consumed it and my mind worked to process it.

On the ride back home that day, I thought about what my neighborhood was missing and why it was missing those things. I wondered if healthy and fresh fruits in schools were a luxury for the more fortunate. Sure, our parents could go shopping and buy these things for the house, but these preppy and destined-for-Ivy-League kids had them at school.

I didn't want to be vegan or go organic. I was 12. I didn't even fully understand what those things were at that age. However, I did want the freedom to make a choice. I also knew I—we—deserved better.

Back at the Avenue Market, whenever I ordered a breakfast sandwich or a chicken box, I started eyeing the grease soaking through the wrapping a little differently. The same with the cheesesteaks I would get from Santa Maria's on Fremont Avenue. And at home, the large can of Crisco my stepmom Barbie used to fry mouthwatering pork chops and roast beef began drawing a few more curious looks. There was a quiet shift happening inside me—a growing curiosity, a subtle questioning of why things were the way they were.

I couldn't help but think about what it was like at The Park School. I wondered what the kids ate for breakfast, and even what the ducks were doing while I was away. It was a moment of realization—not that I wanted to change everything—but I began to see the contrast and felt the weight of what I had been missing, even if I couldn't quite yet articulate it. I knew that everyone in the world wasn't eating just hood food.

CONCRETE RAPUNZEL
by Denim Fisher

When two worlds collided,
I expected a volcano.
In my steady tower
I internalized two realities.
I was molded
To challenge the status quo.
In the latter years of my childhood,
Marble Hill was where I was raised—
A walking Civil Rights Legacy,
Rich history erased by ignorance.
Mama told me not to tell the suburban kids where I lived.
She wanted a better life for me.
Green grass, gifted classes, no distractions.
I was offended,
Because denying my reality—
The hood, where I was embraced—
Meant erasing all the great things
That took place in Druid Heights.
She sent me to this upper-class town.
To get a "good education,"
White lies and tight postures
Them crooked leaders didn't believe in us—
I searched for my education.
It did not arrive on my doorstep.
I sought the truth
Instead of drawing conclusions.
Squares could have boxed me in

But I'm Upton's finest —
I fought my way out
The Black folks I knew
Judged the drug users on Pennsylvania Avenue.
Saying, "They need to clean up the streets."
I believe they didn't choose their reality.
People have a story
Before one is written for them.
Chuck it to the leaders.
Who deprives our neighborhoods
Because of our skin.
Living in two societies
Builds a consciousness
That will never be borrowed from a curriculum.
I looked to the sky,
Even when I didn't see the sun.
Why did we send our youth to the suburbs instead of loving each other?
When will we take the pen back and open the cupboard?

THE BAKE

D ays before the symbolic resurrection of Jesus, my usual question would ring off to my Dad.

"Dad, can you get me something to wear for Easter?" I asked, knowing we really ceased celebrating the Christian holiday.

One reason I figured my Dad, the head of our household, stopped celebrating Easter was heading to middle school and dressing up was something for little kids. The typical fashion of that time was a two-piece suit for boys or at least some slacks, a button-up shirt and a brightly colored, bouncy dress for girls. That fashion was for the house of the Lord. However, for us older kids, the attire changed when it was time to go to the Easter parties or kiddie discos as they called them.

In those venues, kids were fresh from head to toe in Jordans, Nike, Guess and all kinds of designer brands.

But when it came to Easter, my father couldn't have cared less, and his reasons were deeply personal. "Rabbits don't lay eggs," he'd say, brushing off the holiday's traditions. He didn't believe in some white man coming to save us, had no interest in spending money, and, truth be told, we weren't exactly churchgoers. Ours was a household of quiet believers—we'd pray over meals now and then, show up for funeral services and keep a Bible on the accent table in the living room, its cover uncracked and likely gathering dust.

Still, I wanted new clothes to make it feel like a celebration, to blend in with the status quo and create my own version of Sunday service. I wanted to hit the mall and then swing by Shake & Bake Family Fun Center—known colloquially as 'The Bake'—to show off for the girls.

It was tradition, and I wasn't ready to let that go as Dad did, not just yet. So, off to Mondawmin Mall we went to pick up a matching jean jacket and pants set, paired with fresh white sneakers. I was the department store mannequin in Black boy form.

My dad had a signature gold-crowned tooth—one he'd had since he was a preteen—a head thinning toward baldness and a pocket full of cash. He footed the bill at the register, his face emotionless, glancing at me briefly before looking back at the neatly placed bills on the counter. His reluctance was clear, even without words.

Back home, I got dressed, checked myself in the bathroom mirror for the hundredth time and doused myself in some of Dad's most expensive cologne. Finally, I was ready to take the bop up Pennsylvania Avenue toward The Bake. My older cousin, Rob, joined me for the walk. He lived in east Baltimore but spent summers at my house—eating up all the food, hogging my video games, blasting his annoying country music and occasionally messing with my friends. He was basically a pseudo-Deebo from Friday—big and brooding, with a flannel shirt like a uniform and a stare that made people move without him saying a word.

Still, I looked up to him. Wanted to be just like him. A sports lover, I admired the way he threw a football with perfect velocity and spin, just like Brett Favre, his quarterback. And whenever he talked about high school—or more specifically, his "experiences" with girls—I was all ears. I never bothered verifying the validity of his stories, but they were so wild and intriguing if he told me he'd slept with every member of Destiny's Child, I probably would have believed him.

"I had a threesome one time with two girls, and… the other time, I climbed through her window when her parents weren't home… we were in the backseat of her mom's car…" I swear, to my 11-year-old ears, the stories were worthy of a Pulitzer Prize-winning book or an Academy Award-winning movie.

We were meeting my godbrother, Tyrik, who had an arcade-worthy video game collection; his friend Avery, who lived in his apartment building on Callow Avenue; my best friend and classmate Melvin; and a couple of other guys from the neighborhood. Like any great clique in history—Pinky and the Brain, the Teenage Mutant Ninja Turtles, Ed, Edd n Eddy—we were clear on our mission, even without really discussing it in detail.

The Mission:

1. Get 10 numbers and freak (dry hump) at least 50 girls.

2. If Li'l Romeo or Li'l Bow Wow show up, rob one of them (Rob's personal mission).

3. Mean mug any guy lookin' at us for longer than one second.

4. Make sure #3 gets followed early and often.

The line outside The Bake snaked from Pennsylvania Avenue all the way around the block to McMechen Street

"Niggas ain't gettin' in the back of this line. Fuck that!" Rob said, shaking his head as he scanned the sea of kids flexing every designer brand known to man. I walked the line, hoping to spot someone I knew who could help us jump ahead.

"Yo, we up here!" Tyrik yelled, saving the day and calming down "Baby Debo."

The crowd of kids side-eyed us as we jumped the line, but we ain't care. Everybody else was doing it anyway. Nobody was out there regulating the line until a fight broke out around the 130-person mark.

I barely caught what happened before fists started swinging, hair started flying and cops started swarming. Cops were like uniformed roaches in the hood—silent, unseen but always lurking. They moved fast, putting illegal choke holds on the young brawlers and slapping cuffs on them without hesitation.

"Damn, they spent all that money on clothes, hair and haircuts, and still didn't make it in," Tyrik said, laughing at the chaos.

Unfortunately, fights at The Bake weren't anything new. They were an annual tradition, almost like WrestleMania with Bret Hart facing off against 'Stone Cold' Steve Austin. The cops were onto it, too, and parked right across the street, just waiting for the violence to break out.

You'd think they'd try something more proactive, like offering anger management classes or stepping in before things popped off. But nah. Cuffs, backseats of police cruisers and paddy wagons were the go-to, crime-stopping solutions in the hood. I tried to stay clear of it all because I didn't want to call Dad from Central Booking for nothin' stupid, but hands would fly for respect if needed.

By the time we reached the front door, I could already hear the bass booming and smell that funky hot dog aroma that always lingered around The Bake. Security was posted at the entrance, cracking their knuckles, ready to tackle a kid at a moment's notice—just like their cop counterparts.

Once we walked into The Bake, the bowling alley was to the right, down the stairs, and the skating rink was straight ahead, through two large doors on the left. After we paid the entrance fee, we walked through

those big doors like Sincere and Tommy in Belly —
slow motion in our minds, heads high, bathed in low
light like we were the stars of our own classic movie.
The dim glow only added to our mystique as we made
our way to the wall enclosing the skating rink, ready to
make our mark.

Usually, I'd head to the arcade to play Marvel vs.
Capcom or that driving game where you could pop a
wheelie by double-tapping the gas. But today wasn't
about fun—we had business to take care of. We
wanted no prizes produced by tickets and tokens. Our
eyes were dead set on the girls. Phone numbers, hugs,
kisses—every interaction meant something to us young,
hormonal boys with something to prove. The Bake was
our battleground, the place where we came to solidify
our names.

Easter at The Bake always started with casual
skating—some kids skated backward and did spins,
syncing their movements to the music—but it quickly
turned into a dance contest and, eventually, a full-
blown freak fest. We were there mostly for the freak
fest.

At a certain point, the skating session would end,
and skaters would make their way to the concrete wall
circling the rink. They'd plop down at the seats near
the lockers, untie their skates and hand them back to
the attendant who would give them a quick spray with
disinfectant before putting them back on a shelf. The
germs might've died, but the funk always remained.

Sometimes, if we got a whiff of something foul before

lacing up, we'd ask for extra sprays—or better yet, a different pair altogether. Now that I think about it, maybe that was where the hotdog aroma really came from.

Next, the DJ queued up club mixes from Baltimore legends like DJ Rod Lee and DJ K-Swift. Harlem shakers would burn through 500 calories during the dance contests—twisting, popping and moving with unbridled energy, their faces locked in mean mugs—becoming musty, drenched in sweat and possessed by the music.

We watched but never joined. We weren't dancers. We were observers of the scene, watchers of the happenings who played our positions. Girls loved dancers and respected their effort and style, but that just wasn't us. A two step was the most you would find us doing.

After the dance contests ended, we began moving toward the skating rink. As we walked in, the guys were eyeing the girls, and the girls played it cool, acting like they didn't notice all the attention, but they knew they were the trophies we wanted to hoist when the night was over.

"Rob, you still robbin' Li'l Romeo if he shows up?" I asked, smirking with a sly look. Rob nodded, then opened his left palm and repeatedly punched it with his right fist. Everybody laughed hysterically.

"Let's spread out and come back together," Tyrik said, eyeing a light-brown girl like she manifested from a romantic fantasy he envisioned.

"We'll check in later to see who freaked the most girls and got the most numbers."

We all dapped up and started claiming our territory inside the rink. Rob and I took the north side. Tyrik and Avery went east and Melvin and some of the other neighborhood guys took the west.

A few minutes after linking up with Rob, I realized I should've rolled with some of the other guys. Rob wasn't really there for the girls. He was three years older than us, so to him, they were all too young. He was there to look tough—that's about it.

"Go ahead, do your thing, LA. I'll be over here," he told me after I tried to get him to step off the wall and scope out some girls on the dance floor.

My first grinding session was with Tasha. We both attended William Pinderhughes Elementary School, and I swear she had been checking me out since I transferred there from Hilton Elementary a couple years ago. The dance proved it. She threw her ass on me like she was ready for us to be 11-year-old parents. I held my ground, feet anchored firmly, refusing to be moved as she pounded against my pelvis. This was more than a physical encounter—it was a rite of passage in the hood. If you needed support, your homies would step in, bracing your back to help you savor the moment—'I got your back' personified in real life.

In that moment, I thought about what my Dad might

say if he saw me striving to keep my balance during this freak session. Would he applaud his son, shake his head, give a nod of approval, or pull me off the dance floor for forsaking the family name.

Twenty or so minutes later, I walked over to where Tyrik and Avery were. They were bragging about all the girls they'd freaked and the three numbers each of them had grabbed. Basically, they were in the "Hall of Fame," and I was a rookie just joining the team. They were a year older, and I remembered the time at Tyrik's house when he casually told me he'd been the lookout while Avery had sex with a girl in the basement of their apartment complex, down where they did laundry. They were clearly more experienced in courtship than me.

"I hear y'all. I'm about to grab something else," I said, leaning in close since the music was blasting, trying to play it cool but low-key embarrassed that they'd made so much progress in so little time."

My boyhood was now on the line. I needed bodies and numbers—bodies to grind on these Guess jeans and numbers to fill up the folded, lined paper in my front, right pocket.

After a couple of rejections from girls who would rather dance with their friends than with boys, I finally connected with a short girl named Shantay. She didn't gyrate on me too much, but I still managed to get her number. She was a little older than me and went to Mount Royal Middle School. After I slipped her number into my pocket, she kissed me on the cheek and went back to dancing with her friends.

Moments like these were what boys yearned for. Attention from girls in the form of dry humping, phone numbers, hugs, kisses and even sex felt like validation, a stamp of success in our climb toward manhood. Or at least what we thought was manhood. I wish I could've captured the moment, framed it and walked around the skating rink proclaiming, "Here is the boy who got kissed by a girl who left lip prints on his left cheek."

In that moment at the skating rink, I felt like "the man."

But when I looked around, none of my boys had seen it. Her lip-glossed lips pressing against my cheek became a moment only I could savor. And since no one else saw it, no one would believe me if I told them. So I kept it to myself.

If I couldn't prove it, it didn't exist. That's just how it went.

I could've kept going, but the relentless prowl in me was fading, plus, walking back and forth in a crowded skating rink for hours was exhausting. I walked back over to Pseudo-Debo and told him about my adventures. He nodded and asked what time I'd be ready to go. I guess, since Li'l Romeo wasn't showing up, he was ready to disappear. I'm not sure he would have actually fought the young New Orleans rap star, but we would have reminisced about that story forever if he did.

Using some kind of telepathy, the whole crew met in the middle of the rink before heading out to debrief on the mission. Rob and I were in last place with bodies and numbers. Tyrik and Avery were in the lead with about six each. Melvin and his crew were close with four.

Melvin was my best friend, but he wasn't a fan of Rob ever since Rob pushed him around one day when we were playing in front of his house. Melvin's mom came outside and fussed at Rob, telling him to leave Melvin alone. When she went back in, Rob joked about how we heard a bunch of clicks and clacks, like she was locking ten different bolts behind the door. I tried not to laugh when Rob brought it up. I failed every time.

"I was doing me with my guys from The Avenue. We saw y'all a couple times—you probably just ain't see us," he said.

I knew what he really wanted to say was, "I ain't hanging with you while you're with your cousin. He get on my damn nerves."

After our huddle in front of The Bake, we headed out before the swarm of kids started flooding from the building. A dap and a quick "I'll get up with you" was our send-off before we went our separate ways.

Rob and I started walking back to my house. Before

we hit the corner, Tyrik yelled out, "Rob, when we come next year, who you gonna rob?"

Everybody burst into laughter again. Rob just shrugged and gave a quick smirk—like he had no clue but was ready for whomever.

A LESSON LEARNED

The Connection

I met Brittany online, either on BlackPlanet or Myspace, two of the most popular social media platforms of my teenage years. Both platforms turned kids into part-time web developers. We used HTML and basic code to embed music and design eye-catching pages, and we sometimes even helped each other build them from scratch. We were web designers in training.

In the basement of my house in northeast Baltimore's Cedonia neighborhood, I was scrolling through the social media streets when I stumbled on the profile of a thick, curvy, light-brown girl named Brittany. From her page, it was clear she loved taking pictures, and her jeans hugged her body like she wanted the world to notice. She posed in her bedroom, on the block and with her homegirls—who I already knew I'd try to hook up with Melvin and Khalil sooner or later.

"So wassup, you got a boyfriend?" I messaged her directly, skipping the small talk and cutting to the chase. She replied that she was single, but honestly, I didn't care too much about her relationship status. If she was willing to reply—even if she had a man—it probably wasn't as strong as ol' boy thought it was.

"Let's meet up. I be over west and it looks like you stay over there, so we can meet up at the Avenue Market," I told her before asking for her number. She slid me the digits and obliged. I smirked before locking her number in my phone and logging off. Spinning around in my rolling office chair, I yelled out, "Yes sir! I got her!"—glee dripping from every syllable as I smiled to myself.

Later that day, I was on the phone with my cousin Li'l Anthony, one of my father's brother's sons. He and I went to Furman L. Templeton Middle School together for about a year before he transferred. We hadn't talked much since then, so it felt good to hear his voice when he called the house phone asking for me.

When Li'l Anthony talked, you could hear his smile in his voice and his words came out slow, relaxed, and unbothered. It was like talking to rapper Mase.

"How you been, cuz?" he asked.

"I been coolin'. Enjoyin' this summer break so far. Making moves, you know. I also just booked this bad one named Brittany."

"Brittany who?"

"Jones. Brittany Jones."

"She got a gap? Thick? Light-skinned?"

"Yeah—how the fuck you know all that? You hit?"

"Nah, I know her from 'round the way. I ain't never messed with her. I just know who she is and who she be with."

"Bet. I'm linking with her tomorrow. She meeting me up the Avenue Market. I'ma go see my homeboys first, then meet up with her for a minute."

"Oh shit. Tell her I said wassup. She should remember me."

"Say less. I got you."

We talked a few more minutes and then ended the call.

The Link

There was a ritual we had whenever we were getting ready to meet girls—whether we found them online, through the Baltimore chatline or from a homeboy who had a girl with a friend. Like wolves, we moved in a pack, always on the hunt together.

For example, back when I was talking to Shantia, like any good wingman, I made sure to ask if she had a friend for one of my guys. That's how my godbrother, Tyrik, got connected with her godsister, Sarai. I also ended up talking to Alexis—my brother, Tory's, girlfriend's older sister— after he threw me the alley oop. We moved like that. A score for one of us was a score for all of us.

It didn't always play out the way we hoped. Sometimes the friend wasn't quite what we expected—like that scene in Friday when Smokey thought he was meeting Janet Jackson and the woman showed up looking nothing like the actor and R&B singer. But we rolled the dice every time because that was how we played the game. And like any game, you had to play to win.

To gather the wolfpack, I went back to my old block in Sandtown and linked up with Melvin, Bradley and Khalil. Brittany had already heard about them from our phone conversations leading up to the meetup.

"Wassup, Birttany? You got some friends? They pulling up when you meet up with my man LA?" Melvin had asked her more than once. She'd just laugh and say, "We'll see." And today, the homies wanted to find out if she was really gonna come through.

They also wanted to meet the girl who had me cheesin' on the house phone and stepping off to the side to talk on my Motorola i730. And, of course, they wanted to see if her social media pics matched up in real life. Hell, I did too.

We sat on Melvin's steps for a minute, catching up and cracking jokes, then headed out on foot toward the subway station—ready to see what the day had in store.

"She better be bad, yo. Don't have us going to meet no dusty chick," said Bradley.

I think Bradley was a year older than us, or at least that's how he carried himself. He had that natural big brother vibe—laid-back, but you could tell he knew how to make moves on girls. Khalil, like Melvin and me, talked to a lot of neighborhood girls. We even went to a church lock-in once at a church near Lafayette Square. The lack of adult supervision let us do whatever we wanted in the community building across the street from the house of the Lord. I can't remember if we prayed for forgiveness afterward, but it was one of those nights you'd never forget.

"Nah, she right. Melvin saw her. He know what it is," I said.

"Nah, she look cool. I peeped her page online. She was too thick," said Melvin.

"Like your sister?" Khalil replied.

"Stop fucking playing with me, yo," Melvin shot back, quick and direct.

We all burst out laughing as we walked up Fremont Avenue.

On the trek, I remember passing Fat Troy's house. Kids were playing in the alley near his front door. Then we walked past Ron's house. His front door was the color of fresh blood—bright red and impossible to miss.

A bit further down, we passed the office building where we used to ring the doorbell and run after school when we were in third or fourth grade. I don't think anyone ever came out. And if they did, they never caught us—our Nikes were always in sport mode. The thrill of the imaginary chase was worth every sprint.

We passed the Kingdom Hall of Jehovah's Witnesses, boxed in by a massive, black metal fence. I never saw people go in or out, but it always felt protected—not just by the gate, but by God. Everything else in the neighborhood might've been run down—potholes in the street, trash in the gutters, dope fiends asking for change—but that place felt impenetrable.

Just before we hit the corner by the Avenue Market, I called Brittany to make sure she was there.

"I'm out here—where you at? I been waiting for a minute."

"I'm coming around the corner now."

"Oh, I see you."

"I see you, too," I said, a smirk spreading across my face like an infection.

"There he go smirking again—look at yo'," Melvin said, pointing at me, cheesing like crazy, showing all 32 teeth.

The Fumble

I led the pack to the top of the Upton Subway Station where Brittany was waiting in blue jeans that hugged her hips with a kung fu grip. All I could think about was peeling them off her one day—maybe even today, if I played my cards right.

"Finally, boy, you took forever. And you got the whole neighborhood with you," said Brittany.

"Yeah, I had to bring the bros," I replied. "This is Melvin, Khalil and Bradley."

They each gave their usual greetings—slow waves, slight head nods and a "wassup." Melvin, thirstier than the rest, added, "Where ya fine ass friends at?"

His ball cap was cocked to the side, and he wore his usual devious smile he'd mastered ages ago and used to disarm people. Melvin wasn't all games, though—he'd do the dirty work if it needed to be done. He believed in protecting himself and the ones he loved, but he knew how to cut the switch off and turn the charm on when it mattered.

"Oh, you was serious?" Brittany replied. "Sorry, it's just me. And I thought it was just gonna be him," she said, pointing at me. "So I guess we both disappointed," she added with a smile.

"Bitch, stop playing with my man," I blurted. The words flew from my mouth like ninja stars—spinning fast, slicing Brittany right across the face.

My whole crew turned to look at me.

"Chill out, yo—what the fuck?" one of them said.

Brittany looked at me like I'd lost my damn mind.

"What the fuck did you just call me?" she said, eyes sharp with rage, flames replacing her pupils.

Like them, I was shocked at myself. I wondered how I could so easily call Brittany a bitch, without any prompting, agitation or real reason to. As if there was ever really a legitimate reason.

Brittany repeated her question, louder this time.

"The fuck did you just call me?"

Passengers coming and going from the subway glanced over, curious about the commotion. The tension was sharp enough to slice with a Ginsu.

Melvin put his arm around my shoulder and pulled me to the side, Bradley and Khalil trailing.

"Bro, why the fuck you call her that? You gotta chill."

"I don't even know," I said.

By the time we turned around, Brittany was already heading down the stairs of the subway station—catching the train to somewhere else. Somewhere where a boy she'd flirted with for weeks wouldn't randomly disrespect her in front of his friends.

And for what?

Melvin tried to call her back, but she wasn't having it. She paid her fare and walked toward the platform. We started walking back down Fremont, just past the Kingdom Hall.

They kept asking why I said it. Not because the word was immoral, but because I broke the code. I used it out of context. You could say "bitch" in rap lyrics or when describing a girl to one of your boys. Saying things to them like, "I'm bout to go see my bitch," was perfectly fine.

But to say it to a girl's face? That was different. That was not allowed. Also, calling somebody's mom or sister a bitch was fighting words. No debate.

I had fumbled the rock. Violated the rules of the hunt. Broken the pack's code.

"Yo, I don't know what you on, bro. That was the wildest shit I ever seen you do," Khalil said, still laughing in disbelief.

I think I said it to sound cool, to sound like I was in control, to pour some bravado over my nervousness. It was stupid and backfired into my face. I had poured water on the flame I should have poured gasoline on.

And about 21 years removed from the incident; I still reminisce back to that epic fumble. Melvin reminds me of it from time to time, too, whenever we link up. When I think about it, I think about Queen Latifah's U.N.I.T.Y., where she raps, "Who're you calling a bitch?" That line was explosive and direct, coming from a woman who felt highly disrespected. Just like Brittany. The song was so powerful, it won the Grammy for Best Rap Solo Performance in 1995.

I'm not sure if I ever apologized to Brittany. And if she ever reads this, she might say wtf, because this happened decades ago. But still—Brittany, I'm sorry for calling you a bitch that day at the subway station. You didn't deserve that. No Black girl does.

In hindsight, I wasn't just trying to clown—I was trying to perform. Trying to prove something. Maybe I thought it would make me look tough or cool. Maybe I thought the homies would laugh and it would slide. But what actually happened was verbal harm. Embarrassment. Shame. That moment exposed something in me I didn't even know was there.

What really messes with me is how natural it felt in the moment. Like the word was just sitting there, waiting on my tongue. I didn't think. I didn't hesitate. I let it fly like it was mine to use as if it came without consequence.

And that's the part that stuck with me. It's wild how easily boys absorb things—through the environment that we live in—and how slow we are to question them. I had spent weeks getting to know you, hearing your laugh, imagining what it would be like to be around you, curious about what sweet scent you would permeate. Then in less than a few minutes of meeting you, I reduced you to a punchline.

As a 35-year-old man, I think about how that one word—one that gets tossed around like it's nothing—carries generations of disrespect, dismissal and dehumanization. And how it's too often aimed at the very people who love us, look out for us and deserve better from us.

So again, Brittany, I'm sorry. That moment taught me a valuable lesson. And even if you don't remember it, I do. I carry it with me. Because some lessons you don't get to learn without fumbling first.

Tupac's record label released a song called "Never Call U Bitch Again" in 2002 by the late rapper, years after his death. Even in his afterlife, through music, he found a way to show respect to Black women. If he could do it after he was gone, I know I can do it while I'm still here.

Love,

LA

WE FIT THE DESCRIPTION

"What the fuck you looking at?" was all I could think on a summer afternoon as I walked across Mosher Street with Tyrik, Melvin and Eddy as a police officer in his cruiser stared us down like we didn't belong in the neighborhood.

A few moments before "Officer Stare-A-Lot" locked eyes on us, Eddy copped some dime bags of weed and stuffed them like a Thanksgiving turkey in his white crew sock. In the early 2000s, cops weren't hip to checking socks, the perfect stash spot, when randomly stopping and frisking Black people.

I was the connector of my crew — a plug of sorts. Eddy was from Down Da' Hill and spent his summers at football camp, chasing girls, listening to Three 6 Mafia and Bone Thugs-N-Harmony and smoking whatever gas East Baltimore provided, which resulted in his lips turning as black as his skin. We became friends at St. Anthony of Padua, a Catholic school in northeast Baltimore, where we likely helped administrators hit their quota for Black students.

Tyrik was from Callow Avenue in Reservoir Hill. He looked like a younger version of producer Swizz

Beatz, even to the shape of his narrow head, with slightly darker skin and light brown eyes. He was my godbrother, and we were connected since our single-digit years. I spent many nights and days at his house since he had more video games than any person I knew. From The Sims on PC to Ninja Turtles on Nintendo 64, he had nearly every game on every system

I moved to Cedonia when I was about 13, but Sandtown will always be home—that's where I grew up and where I first met Melvin at age 7. We were the same age, but by middle school my faint mustache and goatee made me look older than I really was. His parents were older and less strict than mine, which gave him a kind of freedom I didn't have. He lost his virginity and drank malt liquor well before his teenage years. I'm not saying his parents allowed it, but I imagine the consequences for him weren't nearly as harsh as they would've been for me if I'd come home drunk or with hickeys on my neck.

I brought a Down Da' Hill dude and some guys from other hoods to chill in Sandtown, hanging out and blowing trees. It made me feel like a legend. We were headed to the Upton subway station, on our way to Security Square Mall to meet up with Shantia, a gorgeous, light-brown girl with a jaw-dropping smile I met online. She had friends for the homies, too.

Though they were spread throughout the city, there weren't many differences in Baltimore hoods. They all had dope boys, poverty, drug addicts, terrible schools, vacant homes, too many police, a lot of misguided love and decades of trauma and disinvestment. Even so, those of us from those hoods still, somehow, found ways to separate ourselves.

"Y'all ain't moving no fucking work over here" said Ed, as we walked the scorching block, headed to the Upton subway station. He and Melvin used to always go back and forth about whether east or west Baltimore was more notorious for shit that plagued our communities.

"Boy, you stupid. We move work on this side. Fuck is you talkin' 'bout?" replied Melvin. Every time we linked up, they kept me laughing and shaking my head with their random hood debates.

The jokes stopped when we crossed Mosher Street, just past the corner store where two dollars could get you a Cream soda, Nacho Cheese Doritos, a Star Crunch, and a few Peanut Chews. The officer who had his eyes locked on us hit a U-turn and drove towards us while a second police car sped from an alley like Batman. Seconds later, a third police car appeared out of nowhere. Cops were all over the hood in cuts and crevices, like roaches, in marked and unmarked cars, so ain't no telling where this third pig had been hiding.

"Get your hands up now!" the alley officer yelled after jumping out of his cruiser, pistol drawn. This cop was closest to me, maybe 10 feet away, with his firearm pointed right at me. Fearing the worst, I threw my hands up and froze.

"Get down on the ground, now!" yelled the same

officer. He was the HPIC (Head Pig In Charge). All the cops had their guns pointed at us by now, but he was the only one talking.

We followed orders and quickly made our way to the pavement while keeping our hands extended in front of us like we were doing a yoga move. They didn't handcuff us, though. They didn't have to. A few pounds of trigger pressure could end us. That type of dominance— the kind that determines if you make it to your high school graduation, make it to manhood, make it to your bed or to a casket — was more effective than any handcuff could ever be.

There was a weird calmness among us. We went from coppin' weed and laughing about random hood stories to the most well-behaved and orderly people in the world. We were trained to be subservient when police were around. Parents told us to be wary when they entered our domain. Teachers told us to wave at officers and thank them for their service when we saw them on the street. The streets were filled with stories of the "Wicked Cops of the West" who broke jaws, broke into homes and broke laws. We were hypnotized by their Maryland-flag encrusted badges, the red and blue flashing lights of their vehicles that amalgamated symbols of danger and tranquility and the thought of being a dead nigga in the street.

A few years prior, before I moved to Cedonia, I had watched the police chase and beat a disabled Black man in the alley behind my North Arlington Avenue apartment. The "perpetrator" had a pirate hook instead of a left hand and walked with a consistent limp. That didn't stop one cop from smashing his face into the rocky pavement. No one saved the one-handed man. No was going to save us either.

While my friends were as respectful as students who got called into the principal's office, internally I battled with indignation and inquisitiveness. The sunbaked asphalt pressed against my face, and all I could think about was the one-handed man who'd experienced similar treatment some years prior. It was my turn for this cruel and usual rite of passage. I wanted to get up and yell, "Why the fuck are y'all stopping us? We ain't doing shit," but I refrained from emitting a Samuel L Jackson tone and decided to calmly ask the officers why they were detaining us.

"Your man right here fits the description of someone who was reported to be walking around with a gun in this neighborhood" said the HPIC, finally placing his firearm back inside its holster. Then, he proceeded to tell us a white tee and khakis were the outfit of the supposed gun wielder who was running around Sandtown terrorizing people.

This was 2004. Every Black boy in every Baltimore hood had a white tee. Southern rap artists like Jeezy, formerly known as Young Jeezy, T.I., and Dem Franchize Boyz made them the wave, and my closet was packed with them—just like my friends'. They cost about five dollars, matched almost anything, came in every size imaginable—including the 3X I was rocking—and were easy to find at gas stations and corner stores.

Lord only knows how many Black boys faced our fate that day.

After the cops finished feeling us up and down like club bouncers, they gave us some yellow pieces of paper describing why they stopped us. I guess they were receipts for making us plank on the ground while we got treated like criminals – sort of like our freedom papers.

The yellow slip of paper listed a number to call to file a complaint or ask for more information, but I already knew everything I needed to know. No phone call was going to bring justice—no reparations for me or my friends. We weren't exceptions today. We were disposable. Just boxes to check, lint in the pockets of a system that never thought twice about throwing us away.

Tyrik "fit the description," and that was that. So I tossed the paper into the nearest gutter, we got back on our feet, brushed ourselves off and kept boppin' toward the subway station.

THE FINAL TALE

You don't remember me BJ, but I remember you.

I remember getting my beard trimmed and my hairline chiseled from my barber and mentor, Jabari, at Conscious Heads Barber Shop and Natural Hair Salon, and hearing the creak, groan, and jangle of your horse carriage signaling your arrival. From the large window behind Jabari's barber chair, I'd watch you hop down, check the horse if needed, and situate your assortment of purple and green grapes, ripe cantaloupe, fresh bananas and juicy watermelon. The sounds of your emergence hovered over buzzing clippers, raucous laughter and lively debates. You rode that carriage like a chariot, a gladiator from the garden.

You'd open the screeching screen door and then the second door and walk up the narrow stairwell into the barbershop where your customers waited. "I got fresh fruit outside. Everything sweet, too", you'd say, even offering the shop occupants free samples. "You want to taste something? I got you."

Clothes sweaty from the summer heat, you wore no designer brands—just casual jean shorts and T-shirts most days, sometimes jean overalls. You walked the checkered tiles, spreading your gospel of fruit. Sometimes I got grapes, just like Jabari—your usual stop for a long chat. A local organizer and business owner, Jabari seemed to know everyone, from neighborhood folks to city politicians, and today was no different.

"How you been, man, you alright out there? Jabari would ask, conducting a vibrating chorus of sharp teeth while hair flickered from the fan that blew just in front of his station where you stood.

"I'm alright, but it's crazy out here, man. Guys tried to rob me a li'l while ago."

You'd say it emotionlessly, almost as if it was expected.

The normalcy of the dangerous stories you recalled always captured some laughter. It was a Black barbershop, after all. A place where brothers could talk freely outside the gaze of the larger society.

"Damn, they pulling straps on the fruit man?," another barber yelled, his laughter intertwined in his words.

You'd always be cool about it, though. I think the jokes helped you find some joy in the long days you had as an arraber. From hauling and stacking fruit, to tending to the horses, to offering excellent customer service, to entering the city's most dangerous, underserved neighborhoods—even on the summer's hottest days—I could hear the fatigue in your voice.

Your words were solemn, almost hollow, yet you still managed a sincere smile.

As a child, I lived a few years of my childhood on North Arlington Avenue, just a few blocks away from where the arraber horses were stabled. I don't remember seeing you on a horse and carriage back then. You were probably way too young. But I remember other guys navigating through urban streets with no GPS, steering massive horses, feeding them sugar cubes for sweet treats in the summer heat and yelling out, "Watermelonnnn...canaloooope", their mouths a natural bullhorn, stretching and projecting the words throughout the avenues, roads and boulevards they traveled. When the horses stopped on the corner of Arlington and Mosher, my friends and I would stare in wonder. There was something about a 900-pound animal standing peacefully in a bright red harness, decorative drapes and ornamental bells that intrigued us.

Once, we walked up to one, interested but terrified, our hearts fluttering as we dared each other to get closer.

"You move up."

"No, you move up."

"You scared?"

"No, I ain't scared. Watch this."

Then, once we were a few inches away, the gigantic horse let out a sputtering sound, flapping its lips like a child making silly noises. We all jumped back, simultaneously scared and amused. It was childhood personified.

Last week at a work event for CHARM, a nonprofit that helps young Baltimore writers find their voices and use literature as their bullhorn of truth, I was sitting on the second floor of Blue Pit BBQ eating a barbecue jackfruit sandwich and sipping a turmeric old fashion when the husband of one of my coworkers mentioned your name.

"BJ"

When he mentioned your name, I didn't recognize it at first, because to me you were always just the fruitman. He spoke of your passion for being an arraber and how you were likely the last one doing it I told him about my passings with you at the barbershop, how you always had stories, how your life could be a television show called "The Real True Life of a Baltimore Arabber" and how it'd be a hit. From robberies and fights to stories about your colostomy bag, you never had a shortage of fables to share.

I told the guy how I once taught the daughter of an arraber when I was a fifth grade teacher at Southwest Baltimore Charter School. She even tried to get her father to come to the school to fight me, claiming I yelled in her face when all I did was ask her to stop talking across the room. She spun the whole thing into a tale of public humiliation, and he believed her for a while. Thankfully, the truth came out before I had to square up with her pops.

Last I heard, she was at Temple University in Pennsylvania, doing well for herself. And despite our rocky past, I felt proud. She was chasing her scholarly ambitions, carving out a future beyond what the streets offer. Like the arrabers in her lineage, she wanted more for herself—just like you, just like all of us who come from the depths of Baltimore City.

You don't know this because our barbershop conversations never really touched on my personal life, but I often step away from social media to clear my mind and stay present. According to an August 2025 survey by the American Psychiatric Association (APA), 32% of U.S. adults said social media has done more harm than good for their mental health. Social media is addictive, and I try not to be addicted to anything, so I disconnect to maintain control. I was off Instagram for a few weeks before I returned to the algorithmically addictive streets.

When I returned to Instagram, I came across you on my feed. But you weren't settling your horse or promoting your fruit this time. You were lifeless beside the Upton Subway Station, your blood soaking into the warm pavement. A crowd of angry bystanders surrounded you—screaming, restless, vengeful— wondering why another Black man had been killed by the same police department sworn to protect them. It seemed the Baltimore City Police Department had failed us again.

I clicked the video on the Baltimore Murder Ink page to see what happened. I've seen dead bodies online, in video games, in movies—but it hits your soul differently when the body belongs to someone you know. Someone you dapped up. Someone you shared a laugh with. Someone you were just talking about a few days ago at Blue Pit BBQ.

Your breathless shell, and the blood that spilled from it, was blurred out. It reminded me of the bleeped-out curse words on the 92Q radio station. Listeners always know what words to fill in.

When I was a fifth-grade teacher, I used to teach my students about context clues and how to make inferences—how you need evidence, what you see and hear, and background knowledge, what you already know, to connect the dots, solve the riddle or make an educated guess.

I didn't need the unedited video. I could see through the blur. I knew what had happened there, even without every fine detail.

"Remember the fruitman who used to come to the shop, the one with the wild stories of survival while working around these streets," I said after I called Jabari and he answered the phone, his voice still warming up from his slumber.

"Yeah, of course. What about him?"

"He was killed over by the Avenue Market. The cops shot him. I don't know all the details, but I came across a video on the Baltimore Murder Ink Instagram page that showed him slouched over dead, blood on the pavement, people upset. "It was wild, man," I told

Jabari while sitting on my living room couch. My left hand held my phone, my right propped up my head and my elbow rested on my knee.

"Man, that's crazy. He used to always say it was crazy out there. Did they say what happened, why the cops shot him?

"Nah, not yet. The police should be releasing the footage soon, but of course, you know how they make shit up, stretch the truth, justify the murders. It's crazy how these white boys can shoot up a whole school and get taken alive, not us though. Not us." I said.

Jabari and I talked for a while that day, about you, about life, about the state of our city. We always have these talks, and I always appreciate them. He's no stranger to death as a 50-year-old man who lost his mother a couple of years ago to a health complication. Since then, he's been preaching the gospel of life, trying to get families to reconcile differences, trying to show people we have too much to live for to be beefing with each other. I take heed to his words and try to find ways to incorporate the lessons into my life.

I check in with friends and family members at times, probably not as frequently as I should, to ask if they're okay and whether there's anything I can do to assist. I can always do more, though.

BJ, a few days after I talked with Jabari, I forced myself to sit at my office computer and watch the body cam footage—watch those officers take you from this world. I saw them run up and grab you, not even sure if they announced themselves as police. And I kept asking myself: What made them think this was the way? What convinced them running down on a Black man on Pennsylvania Avenue was the right move?

I wondered if there was another way—if a social worker in a bulletproof vest could've been called. Or one of those crisis negotiators you see in movies, the ones who talk people out of hostage situations. Someone who wouldn't lead with aggression, but with reason. Someone who would try to deescalate. To fight fire with water, just once.

I was recently around the way and heard you had a mental breakdown that day, wanted to end it all, "crashed out," as the kids say. I don't know how true the claims are, but I couldn't help wondering what might have happened, or not happened, in your life to push you there. I also wondered if those days on the carriage ever brought you peace in the middle of the storm, and if that peace had vanished once you stopped riding.

In the end, the officers fired 38 shots at you, BJ—12 fewer than the NYPD fired at Sean Bell after he left his bachelor party. That's three shots fewer than were fired at Amadou Diallo, an unarmed man reaching for his wallet in the Bronx. And it was more than the 8 shots fired at Walter Scott, who was shot in the back while running away in North Charleston, South Carolina. It was also more than the 20 shots in the Stephon Clark case, and more than the three rifle rounds that killed Jordan Edwards, 15, in Balch Springs, Texas—too many others whose names are now stitched into the same blood-stained narrative.

Your murder alone was tragic enough, but where it happened made the pain even heavier. They killed you right outside the Avenue Market, where I learned the taste of a bacon, egg and cheese sandwich, where chicken boxes and half-and-halfs weren't just food but a ritual, and where I found delight in Pokémon cards. Across the street is William Pinderhughes, where I went from third to fifth grade, where I built friendships and was embraced by caring teachers. Just down the block was the convenience store where I bought my first bootleg CD, Fat Joe's Jealous Ones Still Envy J.O.S.E.—a celebratory moment for a Black boy in the hood. A block away is Shake & Bake, where I honed my craft of courting girls. And only a few feet from where you fell is the spot where I disrespected Brittany, calling her out of her name and embarrassing myself in front of my boys, proof that I still had much to learn in the art of seduction. You died at the center of so many of my childhood memories, and now that ground is consecrated as a monument of mourning, replacing the positive memories that once lived there.

If I let the comment section of the news outlet that aired the footage tell it, you deserved to die. If I listen to them, your wielding of a firearm was your death sentence. If I let them remain the dominant narrative, every bullet that entered your body was necessary, justified and required.

They intentionally forget Dylann Roof, who killed

nine Black parishioners at Mother Emanuel AME Church in Charleston, South Carolina, and was arrested without incident, even taken to Burger King before being booked because he said he was hungry. They ignore Nikolas Cruz, who murdered 17 people at Marjory Stoneman Douglas High School in Parkland, Florida, and was calmly apprehended after walking into a neighborhood. They dismiss Payton S. Gendron, who gunned down 10 Black people in a Buffalo, New York, supermarket yet surrendered after police persuaded him to drop his weapon. They overlook James Eagan Holmes, who killed 12 and injured 70 more in an Aurora, Colorado, movie theater and was arrested in the parking lot without a single shot fired at him.

BJ, I usually skip the comment section because it's filled with people who don't understand Baltimore specifically or Black America more generally. They don't understand that most gun-wielders in the hood aren't doing it for glorification—they do it for protection. They do it out of fear. They don't understand the trauma that comes from growing up without, from having to navigate life without agency, without a sense of power or safety.

BJ, they have no clue. They are trolls, willfully ignorant, gleefully stupid and perpetually miseducated about the lives we live. They say outlandish things just for clicks, engagement and hot takes. It fuels them.

BJ, you were 36-years old—just one year older than me—when you lost your life, your chance, your physical ability to do, think, act or be. Your possibilities were upended. Your story was cut short by 38 shots.

BJ, I know they'll read this. They'll mock you. They'll say what they've been programmed to say. They won't care about the people you touched. They won't care about the families you provided for. They won't care about the importance of the arrabers in Baltimore, how they've been staples in a city that's constantly falling to pieces. During COVID, when so many people were shut in, the Arrabers stepped up—delivering produce, masks and supplies right to people's doors, at a time when business owners and city officials weren't doing enough. And in a city full of food deserts, where whole neighborhoods don't have even one grocery store, arrabers have been filling the gap for generations, making sure folks could still get fresh food when no one else would.

I didn't know you that well, BJ. I don't know what high school you went to. I don't know if you had children, a wife or a home. I don't know what your future ambitions were, if you were on your way to them or needed support to get there. I don't know what stresses plagued you, or what dreams woke you up each morning.

All I know is you should still be here in the physical form, untouched by bullets, with six liters of blood in your body, with your mind and soul intact. If I don't know anything else, I know that, BJ.

Until we meet again,

LA

ACKNOWLEDGEMENTS

Thanks to Albert Phillips Sr. for setting the foundation for scholarship for me. You are also an excellent writer, as evidenced by the essays you post on Facebook and the numerous writings you left around the basement on Sunbrook Avenue that I read in awe because of how well they were written. I am thankful to call you my dad.

Thank you to D. Watkins, the Baltimore legend, who inspired me back in 2014 when you spoke to youth in UMBC's The Choice Program. Your writing made me believe that I had stories worth telling, and you continue to inspire storytellers all over the city.

To my editor, Laurie Willis Davis, you came through in the clutch when I needed you most and did a masterful job of offering advice to make my manuscript into something magical. I am forever thankful for your wisdom and inspiration.

To Morgan Elliott, who designed the book cover, marketing materials, website, and so much more that went into this project, thank you. We have much more to do, and I am grateful to have you to call on to bring my visions to life.

To Nikiea Redmond for laying out the interior of my book with such skill and care.

To Damani Coates and the entire Black Classic Press

family for your support, encouragement, and superb printing services.

Thank you to Jabari Natur and Sista Yaa Kenyatta for the opportunity to work at Reality Speaks Bookstore and Media Center many years ago. Being surrounded by books written by prolific Black scholars meant a great deal to me and grounded me in a consciousness I needed at that time. I will share more about that story in a future book. #SolvivazNationForLife

To David Miller, who gave me the advice to "start writing" when I asked for inspiration to begin my first book. As simplistic as it sounded, it was exactly what I needed to hear. Thank you for encouraging everyone, but especially Black men, to document their stories in a professional and authentic way.

To my classmates and professors at the University of Baltimore, thank you for being some of the first people to read and workshop these essays.

To all the Black writers who craft words that inspire, motivate, educate, and reshape our world into something more profound and empathetic.

To Sandtown and all the neighborhoods that raised me, thank you.

Lastly, to my readers, thank you for giving my second book a place on your bookshelf. I do not take your time or support for granted, and I pray this book was worth every dollar you spent.

ABOUT THE AUTHOR

Albert Phillips Jr. is a Baltimore-based writer and educator whose work thoughtfully explores the rich alchemy of Black life, both past and present. A graduate of Morgan State University with a B.S. in Print Journalism and an M.Ed. from Johns Hopkins University, Albert is currently an MFA candidate at the University of Baltimore. In 2020, he published his acclaimed debut book, Y'all Hiring? The Black Teen's Guide to Navigating Employment. His second book, Where You From? Tales of Sandtown, was released in October 2025. Albert's writing has been featured in Black Enterprise, The Afro, Baltimore Fishbowl, and various other online and print publications.

Learn more at **www.AlbertPhillipsJr.com.**

More from the Author

Y'all Hiring?: The Black Teen's Guide to Navigating Employment

www.ingramcontent.com/pod-product-compliance
Lightning Source LLC
Chambersburg PA
CBHW061749070526
44585CB00025B/2840